Chromatography

Or a Treatise on Colors and Pigments, and of Their Powers for Painters and Artists

By George Field

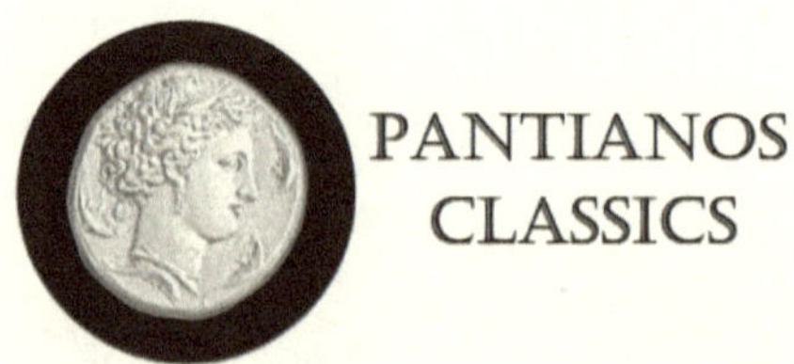

Published by Pantianos Classics

ISBN-13: 978-1-78987-118-0

First published in 1885

Contents

Preface

THIS book is, to some extent, a condensed and revised issue of Field's Chromatography, and is based on the last edition by Mr. T. W. Salter. The work of condensation presented no great difficulty, as a great part of the original volume is taken up by descriptions of pigments never used by artists, and by much irrelevant matter; but the revision was a far more serious task, and in order to bring the work up to date it was found necessary to revolutionize the more theoretical parts, and to write new chapters. [1]

In Part One, therefore, a fresh foundation has been laid, in accordance with the modern science of colour, and the whole work has been rearranged upon this basis. Great stress has been laid upon accuracy of nomenclature, and the terms used throughout the book will always be found consistent with their definitions in Chapter Three. The new treatment of the important subject of contrast will, it is hoped, tend greatly to elucidate this much neglected branch of chromatics.

Field's Chromatography has long been among artists the standard work on colours and pigments, although its high price has somewhat limited the circulation. It is believed that its publication in the present form will largely increase its value, and that the great reduction in price will cause it to be far more extensively circulated.

The Editor is greatly indebted to Professor Rood's treatise on "Modern Chromatics." Reference has also been made to the standard scientific works of the day, more especially to the recently published edition of Watts' Dictionary of Chemistry.

[1] Chapters One to Five; and, in the main, Six and Seven.

Note on the Nomenclature Adopted in This Edition

All forms of colour can be expressed by using three terms, just as a solid body may be defined by reference to three dimensions of space.

This being so, it is a matter of some importance that our three terms should be chosen so as to convey as clearly as possible the ideas they represent, and that they should be restricted to the expression ONLY of these fundamental ideas.

It is obvious that we shall have to employ words which have previously been, however loosely, in general use and the main object, in choosing them for use in restricted senses, will be to pay as much deference as possible to established usage.

The three terms generally used by men of science are *Luminosity, Purity,* and *Hue;* but in a book intended for artists two of these terms would be liable to misapprehension. Thus by luminosity artists often mean richness of tint, and would certainly be surprised to hear that a colour by admixture with white is diminished in purity.

The terms TONE, TINT, and HUE, have therefore been selected as being, with reference to the above considerations, most suitable to express the respective ideas.

The word TONE is often used to express the idea of luminosity (light and shade), and is largely used by Chevreul in this sense. Thus, in his fundamental definition of "tone". he states that a colour is deepened in tone by mixing it with black.

Again, the word TINT, although often used as a synonym for *Hue,* is very generally employed by artists to express the result of mixture with white. Thus, in oil-painting, the artist forms his "tints" by mixture with white lead; and in water-colour by spreading thin washes on paper: — in both cases the optical result being, in the main, mixture with white light.

Introduction

It is difficult to say when the knowledge of colouring possessed by the ancients first approximated to a science. We know, however, that they had attained to considerable skill at a very early date.

The paintings of the Egyptians have been much eulogised for brilliant and harmonious colouring, particularly those at the tombs of the Egyptian kings at Thebes. These are often on a very large scale, and are in perfect preservation.

The pigments used by the Egyptians were confined to *red, yellow, green, blue, black,* and *white;* and their chromatic compositions were remarkably well balanced. Indeed, considering the brightness of some of the colours, it is astonishing how well, by judicious contrast, and the skilful use of black, they have succeeded in avoiding a gaudy effect.

The Egyptians paid great attention to the decoration of the walls and ceilings of their houses, and also executed paintings on rolls of papyrus; but their best efforts are undoubtedly those on the tombs and temples.

The Assyrians, as shown by Layard in his discoveries at Nineveh, also possessed a knowledge of colouring. Their pigments were similar to those of the Egyptians, and although very limited, were arranged with taste and skill.

In the paintings of both nations a well-defined black outline was a very characteristic feature.

The Greeks learnt painting from the Egyptians; their colouring reached its perfection under Zeuxis and Apelles, 450 to 350 B.C. After this — about 300 B.C. — art rapidly deteriorated, the invasion of the Romans commenced, and the principles of light and shade, and of colour, as understood by the Greeks were lost, together with their valuable treatises on the subject.

Composition of Pigments used by the Ancients.

Analysis by Sir Humphrey Davy, and by French chemists, has given the following results: —
Egyptian and Assyrian Pigments.

Red. — Ochres and cinnabar (Native Vermilion).
Yellow. — Ochres and orpiment.

Green. — Mixtures of yellow with copper blue.

Blue. — The celebrated "Alexandria blue" (a silicate of copper and lime), and probably also lapis-lazuli (native ultramarine). The latter was perhaps the famous "Armenian Blue" of the ancients.

Black. — Carbonaceous substances and black earths.

White. — Chalk and plaster of Paris.

Greek and Roman Pigments.

Red. — Ochres, cinnabar, red lead, and a pink lake of unknown origin.

Yellow. — Ochres and orpiment.

Green. — Mixtures of yellow with copper blue.

Blue. — "Alexandria blue," lapis-lazuli, and "Indian blue" (Indigo.)

Purple. —"Grecian" or "Tyrian purple" (extracted from a shell).

Brown. — Ochres and Oxide of Manganese.

Black. — Carbonaceous substances.

White. — Chalk.

It will be seen that the above lists are almost entirely made up of mineral substances. In the case of the Egyptian and Assyrian pigments no traces of vegetable colours have been found; although it is highly probable that they originally existed, but have undergone the process of decay to which all organic substances are so liable. It has been shown during the progress of excavation that some of the ancient pigments were certainly not permanent. Certain blues and reds, which were brilliant and vivid when the earth was removed from them, faded rapidly on exposure to the atmosphere.

A considerable amount of information with respect to ancient pigments has been handed down to us by Pliny, in his Natural History, and also by Theophrastes and Vitruvius.

The early Roman and Florentine painters were far behind the Greeks in comprehension of the principles of refined colouring. The partial restoration of these principles seems to have been coeval with the earliest practice of painting in oil. The glory of the revival belongs to the Venetians, to whom the art of painting passed with the last remains of the Greek schools after the capture of Constantinople at the beginning of the thirteenth century. Giovanni Bellini laid the foundation of colouring, and Titian carried it to high perfection.

From the Venetian it extended to the Lombard, Flemish, and Spanish schools.

In the practice of the individual in painting as well as in all revolutions of pictorial art, in ancient Greece as in modern Italy, colouring has been the last attainment of excellence in every school. Although colouring does not constitute a picture, yet it is the flesh and blood that clothes the skeleton of graphic art. Without it the finest performances look lifeless. It was the deficiency of colouring in the great works of the Roman and Florentine schools that caused Sir Joshua Reynolds to confess there was for him a certain want of attraction in them. To relish and truly estimate their greatness required, he said, a forced and often repeated attention; and "it was only those persons incapable of appreciating such divine performances who made pretensions to instantaneous raptures on first beholding them."

Gainsborough also, with a candour similar to that of Reynolds, upon viewing the cartoons at Hampton Court, acknowledged that their beauty was of a class he could neither appreciate nor enjoy.

Of the rank and value of colouring as a department of painting there will be, as there have been, differences of opinion corresponding to differences in the powers of the eye and understanding; but take from Rubens, Rembrandt, Titian, and other great masters the estimation of their colouring, and we fear that what is left to them would hardly preserve their names from oblivion. It is colour which the true artist most loves, and it is the perfection of colouring in all its complexity that he ever seeks to attain.

Part One - On the Science of Colour

Chapter One - On Light and The Production of Colour

Light is the sensation produced by the action of luminous rays upon the retina of the eye.

A luminous ray, so called simply because it produces the sensation of light, is due to the propagation of a wave motion through a subtle, imponderable, and highly elastic medium, called the *Luminiferous Ether,* which surrounds the particles of all bodies and pervades all space.

For the production of the sensation of light in the ordinary way, the following stages of the process have to be considered: —

(1.) **Physical Cause.** — Luminous rays enter the eye and fall on the terminal expansion of the optic nerve which forms a lining membrane at the back of the eye, and is called the *Retina.*

(2.) **Physiological Effect.** — The luminous rays stimulate the retina and give rise to a *sensory impulse.* This sensory impulse is conveyed by the optic nerve to a special part of the brain, and is there transformed into a *sensation.*

Although light must, as above, be strictly defined as a sensation, yet as we have no word by which to designate an assemblage of ether waves, it is usual for convenience to also use the word light in the purely physical sense. Thus a collection of luminous rays which by their action on the retina would produce' the sensation of white, is spoken of as "White Light." And similarly other kinds of rays are named after the sensations they are potential to evoke.

Colour is, like light, a sensation, but in its widest significance (for we are forced to accept black and white as colours) requires an even more comprehensive definition; black being a *negative* sensation produced by the absence of any action of luminous rays upon the retina.

Composition of Ordinary White Light

Ordinary white light — i.e. diffused daylight — is composed of a mixture of an immense number of rays of different wave-lengths, or, what is the same thing, of different *colours,* for colour is an attribute of wave-length. Each of these rays acting singly on the retina would produce in the eye the sensation of a distinct colour; but the fusion of all the sensations generated by the mixture of rays gives the sensation of white.

This compound character of white light can be shown by the action of a glass prism.

The Spectrum. — A ray of light when passed through a glass prism is turned out of its course, or refracted. Now the shorter the wave length of a ray, the more it is *refracted,* so that if we pass a beam of white light through a glass prism, it gets decomposed into its constituent rays, and we obtain the well-known arrangement of colours called the *Spectrum,* with the waves of light classified in order of their wave-lengths. The red rays, which have the longest waves, are at one extremity of the spectrum, the orange rays come next, then the yellow, green, and blue rays; finally, at the other extremity, we have the violet rays, which, having the shortest wave-lengths, are consequently most refracted.

The length of a wave of red light is about thirty millionths of an inch, and of a wave of violet light about fifteen millionths. The intermediate colours of the spectrum have, of course, intermediate wavelengths.

The colours of the spectrum are, both in a physical and in a physiological sense, the purest with which we are acquainted, and hence they are always taken as standards. The colours of natural bodies are never pure; but are always mixed with a larger or smaller proportion of other colours, especially those which are closely allied to them in point of wave-length.

The *Rainbow* is Nature's spectrum on a large scale, and is produced by the action of rain drops on the solar light. A globule of rain, in fact, has a decomposing action similar to that of the glass prism above; but does not perform its analytical office with such exactitude. The differently coloured rays, into which the beam of sunlight which falls on a raindrop is decomposed, emerge from it at different angles. Consequently, all drops at a certain angular distance from the eye send light of a particular colour. We thus obtain the familiar semi-circular band, any radial slice of which is comparable to the spectrum on the frontispiece.

With scientific spectroscopes, furnished with powerful combinations of prisms, the analysis of solar light has been carried to great perfection, and many hundreds of dark lines crossing the spectrum, have been mapped out. These *absorption lines* occur always in exactly the same relative positions. They have been shown to be due to the absorptive action of the sun's atmosphere on the radiation from its intensely heated interior; and have enabled men of science to ascertain, with absolute certainty, the presence there of many terrestrial elements.

The principal absorption lines in the spectrum have letters affixed to them, and are very convenient for reference.

The table on the following page represents, according to Vierordt and Rood, the approximate proportion of chromatic rays in 1,000 parts of White Sunlight.

It is evident, since there is perfect gradation of colour in the spectrum, that the lines of demarcation have to be assigned arbitrarily.

Colours of Natural Bodies

Natural bodies are either luminous, or nonluminous. The luminous ones, such as the sun, the different artificial lights, etc., are seen by the light which they themselves emit. The non-luminous bodies are seen by the light which is thrown on them by the luminous ones, and reflected to our eyes. As the light of the sun in ordinary daylight forms the principal illumination at our disposal, we have explained in detail the constitution of this light; and we shall now show how the colours of natural bodies are produced by its agency.

Red	54
Orange red	140
Orange	80
Orange yellow	114
Yellow	54
Greenish yellow	206
Yellowish green	121
Green and bluish green	134
Greenish blue	32
Blue	40
Bluish violet	20
Violet	5
	1000

Just as when white light is passed through a prism, the colours are a result of its decomposition; so are the colours of natural objects due to the decomposition of the white light that falls on them. And just as each body decomposes light in its own particular way, so does each body exhibit its own particular colour.

Most substances possess a power of what is called *Selective Absorption,* i.e. they have a preference for rays of a certain colour: these rays are absorbed by the substance and extinguished. What is left of the original white light, after this absorption, is what determines the colour of the body.

Suppose we have a piece of red cloth, this is what happens when daylight falls on its surface: — 1st, a portion of the light is reflected from the surface and does not enter the substance of the cloth: this light is scattered irregularly, and is quite unaltered in composition; some of it reaches the eye and dilutes the chromatically coloured light. This is one reason why ordinary colours are never pure like those of the spectrum.

2ndly. The rest of the light penetrates beneath the surface, the process of selective absorption takes place, and all but the red rays are absorbed. As it cannot absorb these, they are reflected back from the interior of the cloth, and reaching the eye of the observer determine its colour.

If the cloth absorbed *all* but the red rays, and we could arrange matters so that no reflected white light from the surface reached the eye, then its colour would be pure as that of the spectrum. As a matter of fact we know of no natural coloured substance which rejects only one kind of ray: there is always an admixture of a larger or smaller proportion of other kinds, which may be revealed by prismatic analysis. This is the principal reason why the natural colours are never pure.

In certain cases the power of absorption possessed by the body is not selective. Some substances absorb *every* kind of ray; hence no light whatever is sent to the eye, and they appear black. Others do not absorb any rays whatever, or absorb them in the proportions in which they occur in the incident white light; such bodies appear white or grey.

It is evident from the above explanation that *no body can exhibit a certain colour unless the rays corresponding to that colour are contained in the light by which it is illuminated.*

Constants of Colour. — It has been shown very conclusively by scientific men that there are three fundamental things on which the colour of a body depends:

1st, its *Purity* (Richness of Tint), or freedom from the sensation of white;

2nd, its *Luminosity* (Tone), or the absolute amount of sensation; this will depend upon the total quantity of light sent to the eye.

3rd, its *Hue,* or that quality of colour which depends upon the wave length of the light

These three things have been called the "Constants of Colour," and by reference to them any known colour may be accurately defined.

Relative Luminosities of Various Colours. — According to Lambert and Professor Rood the substances below reflect the following proportions of daylight incident on their surfaces: —

Polished silver . .	92	per cent.
„ steel . .	60	„
White paper . . .	40	„
Chrome yellow paper .	32	„
Emerald green „ . .	19	„
Vermilion „ . .	10	„
Artificial ultramarine .	4	„

Relative Purity of Various Colours. — Professor Rood states that the colour of paper painted with *vermilion* (as a water colour, in thick paste) contains about 20 per cent, of white light. The colours of *emerald green* and of *artificial ultramarine,* similarly applied, contain about 20 and 25 per cent, of white light respectively.

Colours of Metallic Powders. — These differ from ordinary pigments, firstly in having greater luminosity, and secondly in reflecting light regularly from their particles.

A metallic surface which is very bright in one position will, in another position which is only slightly different, send scarcely any light to the eyes. The alternation of very bright with very dark portions produces a characteristic effect upon the retina.

Transparent and Opaque Substances. — A substance which is perfectly transparent to all kinds of light can have no colour, and in fact would be invisible. Very thin glass approaches this condition.

The difference between transparency and opacity is simply one of degree. Water, one of the most transparent substances we possess, is practically opaque in very thick layers; and gold, one of our most opaque bodies will, when beaten into thin leaves, allow green light to pass. Most substances are more transparent to some rays of light than to others; but this is only stating in another way the fact mentioned earlier, that they have a power of selective absorption. The chromatic colours of all objects seen by daylight must be due to a certain amount of what we may perhaps call "superficial transparency" to particular rays of light.

Artificial Illumination

When pictures painted by daylight are viewed by artificial light, the colours are more or less disturbed.

Gas and Lamplight are very deficient in the violet, bluish green, and blue rays, a certain proportion of which is necessary for the production of white, and so the resultant colour is orange-yellow. Consequently, all the yellows look much the same as the whites, and get taken for whites: the blues turn into greyish blues, etc. The electric light is by far the best form of artificial light, as its composition approximates to that of daylight.

Mixture of Colours

This cannot be effected by mixing pigments. The reason of this will be shortly explained, and in the meantime we shall describe three methods by which a true mixture of colours may be effected.

(1.) **Maxwell's Method.** — One of the best ways of mixing colours is to paint sectors of a disc with the pigments representing them, and cause it to rotate rapidly. The disc will then appear of uniform colour, which is the mixture of the original colours. The proportions of the colours may be varied by varying the sizes of the painted sectors.

This method of mixing colours was described by Ptolemy in the second century. It was much improved by Professor Clerk-Maxwell, who made great use of the "colour-top" in his investigations.

Maxwell's Discs have a slit from the circumference to the centre. This simple and ingenious device enables the experimenter, by overlapping two or more coloured discs, to combine them in any desired proportion. The rotation can be accomplished by adapting a top for the purpose, or by using a rotation apparatus furnished with a multiplying wheel.

(2.) **Lambert's Method.** — A convenient method by which the colours of any two pigments may be mixed, is to paint two surfaces of equal area with them, and arrange these horizontally with a piece of clear glass, held vertically, midway between them. On looking through the glass at one of the colours it is seen to be mixed with the reflected image of the other. As the amount of reflected light increases with the angle of incidence they may be mixed in different proportions by simply shifting the position of the eye, or by moving the coloured surfaces further apart. A black background will be found most convenient for experiments.

(3.) **Mile's, or the Artistic Method.** — The third method is of high value to artists, as it admits of practical application to their pictures. Small spots or thin lines of different colours, placed close together, are blended when the eye is placed at a suitable distance, a true mixture of colours takes place, and a much brighter effect is produced than would have been possible by actually mixing the pigments.

The effects of stippling and of cross-hatching depend on this principle. Ruskin remarks, in his "Elements of Drawing," "Breaking one colour in small points through or over another is the most important of all processes in good modern oil and water-colour painting."

Effects of Mixture of Pigments

It cannot be too strongly impressed on artists that the colour obtained by mixing pigments together is not the mixture of the original colours.

The reason of this was first clearly pointed by Helmholtz in his "Physiological Optics." He reasons as follows: —

"In a coloured powder each particle is to be regarded as a small transparent body which colours light by selective absorption."

"If the colours of powders depended only on light reflected from their first surfaces, the light reflected from a mixed powder would be the sum of the lights reflected from the surfaces of both. But most of the light, in fact, comes from deeper layers, and having had to traverse particles of both powders, must consist of those rays which are able to traverse both. The resultant colour therefore depends not on addition but on subtraction."

Production of Green by Mixture of Blue and Yellow Pigments. — This fact is the strong point of the adherents of the old theory (see Chapter Two.), who regard green as a secondary colour produced by the mixture of blue and yellow. The true significance of the fact forms a kind of *pons asinorum* to the science of colour, which they find utterly impassable.

The artist will be prepared, from the explanation in our last paragraph, to understand that although blue and yellow *pigments* may afford green by admixture, yet it does not by any means follow that the mixture of blue and yellow *colours* will give a similar result.

And it is an established fact that by mixing pure blue and yellow colours in proper proportions, white, or grey (white of low luminosity) is produced, i.e. they are "complementary colours" (see Chap. Two.): and *not by mixing them in any proportions can green be obtained.* Any artist can try the experiment for himself by either of the three methods of colour mixture we have just described.

The green which invariably results when we mix blue and yellow pigments can readily be accounted for as follows:

No natural colour is pure; it is always, as already stated, mixed with a larger or smaller proportion of other colours closely allied in wavelength.

By looking at the spectrum on the frontispiece, it will be seen that green and violet are the colours most allied to blue in point of wave-length.

Therefore blue pigments transmit principally blue; but also green and violet rays.

In the same way, yellow pigments transmit yellow, green and orange rays.

The green rays are the only ones transmitted by both pigments, and hence, when they are mixed, green is the resulting colour.

The more opaque the pigments mixed together the more closely will the resulting colour approximate to that produced by the true mixture of the colours. This accounts for the fact that it is impossible to get a good green by mixing an opaque: blue with an opaque yellow pigment.

Loss of Luminosity by Mixture of Pigments. — It follows from the foregoing principles that when we. mix differently coloured pigments, more or less black is always produced in consequence of absorption. This is borne out by practice: the colour produced by mixture is never so bright as the mean brightness of the original colours, and in some cases the loss of brightness is very marked. This is particularly well shown in the case of vermilion and ultramarine.

If we mix the *colours* of these pigments, by either of the three methods indicated above, we obtain a *brilliant purple;* but by actually compounding the *pigments* we obtain *blackish-gray* as the resultant colour.

If we possessed perfectly pure pigments, i.e. pigments which send light to the eye which is uniform in wave length, then if they were at all transparent the mixture of any two of them in equivalent proportions would produce black, and we could not by mixing them in *any* proportions produce a new colour: the result would always be a shade of that original colour which happened to be in excess.

In so far, then, as the artist depends on the mixture of pigments, it is a matter of congratulation to him that he does not possess them optically pure.

Chapter Two - Theory of Colour

Young's Theory of Colour. — This theory of colour which was first put forward by the celebrated Dr. Thomas Young, and has since been greatly developed by Professor Helmholtz in Germany, and Professor Clerk-Maxwell in England, is now universally admitted.

According to this theory the human brain possesses three primary colour sensations: — *red, green,* and *blue;* and each elementary part of the retina is supplied with three different nerves, which are specially adapted to receive the sensory impulses corresponding to these fundamental sensations. Thus the eye contains three sets of nerves, one of which is specially susceptible to long waves of light, and hence transmits an impulse which gives rise to the sensation of *red;* another is most responsive to the action of waves of medium length, and originates the sensation of *green;* while the third set of nerves is stimulated by the shorter waves, and produces the sensation of *blue.* Furthermore, although each of these three kinds of light acts most powerfully on the nerves specially designed for its reception, yet it also acts to a slight extent on the other two sets of nerves.

Light, the wave length of which is intermediate between the wave lengths corresponding to two primary sensations, acts on both sets of nerves: the extent of the action in each case being proportionate to the relationship in wave length.

The sensation of white is produced when the three sets of nerves are equally stimulated, and the sensation of black when there is no stimulation whatever. Grey is, of course, white of feeble intensity.

This theory has received powerful support from a study of the phenomena of colour-blindness. In the most common form of *colour-blindness* the sensation of *red* is wanting. The most reasonable way of accounting for this, is to assume that the nerves which respond to red light are absent or inoperative; and if we choose red for one of the primary colour sensations, it can be demonstrated that the other two must be green and blue of a violet hue.

The rest of the colours of the spectrum, although excited by rays of only one wave length, are compound colours; because the light, though simple, has the power of exciting two or more colour sensations in certain proportions.

The sensation of yellow, for instance, is produced as follows: — the wave length of yellow light is intermediate between the wave lengths of green and red light, and so it acts both on the red and the green nerves. The mixture of sensations produces yellow. According to this explanation, if we present to the eye a mixture of green and red light, we ought to produce the sensation of yellow. This is readily proved to be the case, and is best shown by mixing the red and green of the spectrum.

Thus we see that, in the case of the compound colours, the same colour sensation may be produced by two totally distinct methods: by the action on the retina of one kind of light, or of a mixture of two different kinds. The unassisted eye is powerless to make any distinction. The difference of physical constitution can, however, be readily detected by the aid of a prism.

The dullness of the yellow obtained by mixing the colours of vermilion and emerald green on the colour top, has been shown by Professor Rood to be due to the following causes:

I. Our ordinary yellow pigments are much more saturated than our red and green pigments, and hence we judge our result by a false standard.

II. Red and green light both act to some extent on the blue nerves, and hence the sensation produced by their joint effect is largely mixed with white. The yellow light of the spectrum and of ordinary yellow pigments, which is simple in wave length, has but little action on the blue nerves and hence produces a more saturated colour.

Primary Colours. — Primary colours may be defined as those which are simple and incapable of being compounded; but which will by admixture yield all other positive colours.

The term Primary Colour is only allowable in the sense of *Primary Colour Sensation:* objectively there can be no such things as Primary Colours. Colour is a sensation produced by a light wave of a certain length, and colour, outside of ourselves, does not exist. In the sense, then, that we have indicated, *Blue, Green,* and *Red,* are the primary colours.

To give exactness to our theory, it is necessary to define the precise hues of these colours. This is always done by reference to the fixed lines of the spectrum. The lines chosen by Clerk-Maxwell are indicated in the frontispiece, and he selected *Scarlet-Vermilion, Emerald Green,* and *Artificial Ultramarine Blue* as their best representatives among pigments.

The Old Colour Theory. — The old theory, which was advocated by Sir David Brewster, states that *Red, Blue,* and *Yellow,* are the primary colours. It is founded on the results of the mixture of *pigments,* and the transmission of light through *coloured glasses,* and is still adhered to by many artists; but with the general progress of scientific education is rapidly losing ground. We explained in the last chapter the difference between the mixture of colours and the mixture of pigments, and precisely the same explanation holds good in the cases where light is transmitted through coloured glasses; the resulting colour, when white light is viewed through a combination of coloured glasses, being what is left of the white light after each of the glasses has absorbed certain constituents, and is therefore not the mixture of the colours of the glasses, as is commonly supposed.

Primary Pigments. — It is an undoubted fact that from mixtures of *red, blue,* and *yellow* pigments, all colours may be approximately produced, and that red, blue, and green pigments would not answer the purpose. And therefore the artist, although he cannot call red, blue, and yellow, *primary colours,* may in the above practical sense term them *primary pigments.* It is however doubtful whether the term "primary pigment" should not be restricted to the sense of "pigment of primary colour."

Colour Diagrams

It is impossible on a plane surface to represent all forms of colour, for as there are three constants of colour we shall require three dimensions of space; but it is possible to do so by means of a solid, such as that formed by joining two equal triangular prisms by their bases. The brightest possible white being placed at the apex of one of the prisms, the darkest possible black at the apex of the other, and finally the three primary colours, in full intensity, at the remaining angular points.

Maxwell's Colour Chart. — (*See front cover*) is the best of the representations on a plane surface. Here the primary colours in full intensity are placed at the angular points of a triangle, and from these the intensity gradually diminishes until it is zero at the opposite sides. The interior of the triangle will contain all possible hues, because within it the three primary colours will be mixed in all possible proportions. The centre of the triangle, containing equal proportions, will be white. Along the sides we shall of course have all the secondary colours: i.e. the mixture of any two primaries in all possible proportions, and finally, colours which are opposite to each other will be complementary in hue.

It will be seen that Maxwell's Colour Chart is a section of the solid described above through a plane parallel to the common base of the prisms. It should be remarked that the chart on the cover is not absolutely true; but is simply a diagrammatic representation of the truth. In a perfect chart the luminosity should be equal over the whole area of the triangle. Such a chart, executed with the brightest of our pigments, would be grey (white of low luminosity) in the centre.

A comparison of our Maxwell's Chart with any of the ordinary red, blue, and yellow arrangements, should appeal to the eye very strongly in favour of Young's theory.

Complementary Colours.

One colour is said to be complementary to another when the mixture of the two produces the sensation of white. Every chromatic colour has its complementary, i.e. certain rays are wanting which if supplied would produce white light.

Negative Images. — If we look steadily at a patch of bright chromatic colour, and then turn our eyes to a white wall, we see what is called a *negative,* or *accidental image,* the colour of which is complementary to that of the original.

This phenomenon is readily accounted for by Young's theory. Suppose we are looking at a red patch. The nerves which are excited by the red rays get tired by the prolonged gaze, and when white light enters the eye their action is greatly weakened: the other two sets of nerves, however, respond fully to the stimulus. Consequently, the balance of action necessary for the production of white is disturbed, the sensations of blue and green predominate, and so we get a negative image of a bluish-green colour.

Sometimes, with extremely bright colours, the accidental image is at first *positive,* i.e. of the same colour as the object; but this appearance, which is due to the persistence of very powerful sensations on the retina, is only transitory, and is always followed by the negative image.

The complementaries to the colours of the spectrum are —

Red	Violet	Purple. [1]
Orange	Bluish green.	Greenish yellow.
Yellow	Greenish blue.	
Green	Blue.	

A knowledge of complementary colours is of great importance to the colourist, as he is enabled by their juxtaposition to obtain his most powerful contrasts of hue.

Effect on Colours of Change of Luminosity

It has been assumed so far that the colour of a body is always the same when seen under the same kind of illumination. This is not strictly the case, for the colour varies, to a certain extent, with the *intensity* of the illumination.

Substances that look red by ordinary daylight will appear orange in bright sunshine; similarly, green will become yellowish-green, and in general all colours become yellower in hue, and paler. Young's theory explains this effect as follows: — As long as the intensity of a colour is moderate it will act almost entirely on its own set of nerves; but when the intensity is great, it acts also on the other sets of nerves, and hence we get change of hue. When the illumination is very intense, all colours approximate to yellowish-white.

These facts have a practical bearing for the artist, for by using pale colours he is able to express high illumination.

When the intensity of illumination is diminished, colours become bluer in hue, and when the light is very feeble all colours tend to shades of blue. The explanation of this is, that the action of feeble light is mainly confined to one set of nerves.

Artists take advantage of this principle in the representation of moonlight effects.

It is evident from the above considerations that a mean degree of illumination is best suited for the differentiation of colours.

Readers who wish to extend their acquaintance with the modern theory of colour, are strongly recommended to read Professor Rood's book on 'Modern Chromatics' in the "International Scientific Series." [2] Those who are specially interested in the question from its physiological aspect, will find an admirable exposition of our present knowledge of the subject in Dr. Michael Foster's classical "Text Book of Physiology."

[1] There is no purple in the spectrum, as it cannot be produced by waves of one kind, whatever their length. It is readily obtained by combining the ends of the spectrum.
[2] Many points have been well touched upon by Mr. John Collier in his "Primer of Art."

Chapter Three - Colour Nomenclature and Classification

We shall now proceed to give some definitions founded on the principles of the last two chapters.

Colour, in its broadest sense, may be defined as the kind of sensation we experience in consequence of:—

I. The composition of the light that affects our eyes.
II. The absence of light altogether.

The 1st class includes white, grey, [1] and the different varieties of chromatic colour. These may be called *Positive Colours.*

The 2nd class contains only black, which being a negative sensation, may be called a *Negative Colour.*

Achromatic Colour is the effect of either —

I. Perfect balance of stimulation of the three set of colour nerves (white and grey) or

II. Absence of all stimulation (black).

Achromatic colours are often called *Neutral Colours* because they are supposed not to change the hue of colours with which they are mixed. The supposition is, however, not strictly correct. We have shown, at the end of our last chapter, that mixture with black, i.e. reduction of luminosity, always changes the hue of a colour.

Chromatic Colour is the sensation produced when the three sets of colour nerves are not equally stimulated. All colours except black, white, and grey, belong to this class.

It will be seen that what we here call "chromatic colour" is theoretically in some cases, and practically in all cases, a mixture of chromatic colour with white of greater or less intensity. But the mixture is always named after the chromatic colour. Thus, what we call blue may really contain only a small percentage of blue rays, the remainder being white light.

Tone. — By the "tone" of a colour we mean its brightness or luminosity, i.e. the total quantity of light it sends to the eye, irrespective of the optical composition of that light. Colours, according to their greater or smaller luminosity, are described as respectively *lighter,* and *darker* in tone.

Tint. — When two colours differ in the proportion of white light they contain, they are said to be of different "tints." According to the larger or smaller proportion of white light present, colours may be described as respectively *poorer,* and *richer* in tint.

Hue is the term which is used for expressing kind, or variety, of chromatic colour. It depends as shown in Chapter One., on the wave length of the unneutralized light.

These three terms — tone, tint, and hue, express fundamental ideas, and it is very important that their meaning should be accurately grasped. The conception of any one of them does not at all involve that of the other two. Thus two colours may be identical in hue, and yet differ both in tone and tint; they may be identical in hue and tint, and yet differ in tone: they may be identical in hue and tone, and differ in tint, etc. etc. To state the case more generally, two colours may differ, or may be identical, in any one, two, or three, of the above respects.

The three definitions may be collected concisely as follows: —

Tone = Absolute quantity of positive colour-sensation, irrespective of its chromatic or achromatic character.

Tint = Relative quantity of positive achromatic and chromatic colour sensation.

Hue = Quality of chromatic colour-sensation.

Luminosity is, as stated above, synonymous with tone.

Shade. — When two colours are identical in hue and tint, but different in tone, that which is darker in tone is called a shade of the other. It will be seen from this definition that "shade" is a restricted sense of "tone."

"Shade" is usually defined as the mixture of a colour with black; but this definition is objectionable, for mixture with black, or reduction of luminosity cannot (see end of Chap. Two.) be effected without, to a greater or less extent, changing the hue of the colour acted upon.

Purity or Richness. — A colour is said to be "rich" or "pure" when the proportion of white light entering into its composition is small.

Saturation.— Depends both upon richness and luminosity. It may be defined as the amount of chromatic colour per unit surface. The distinction between saturation and richness will perhaps be best illustrated by an example.

Suppose (1) a square inch of red surface has a luminosity of 100, and of this 25 per cent. = white light, the remainder consisting of red rays.

Suppose (2) a square inch of another red surface to have a luminosity represented by 300, the radiation consisting of 50 per cent, each red and white light.

Then (2) will be twice as "saturated" as (1), because there is twice as much red light in the same area.

But (1) will be the "richer" of the two colours, because the proportion of red to white light is greater.

Pale and Deep Colour. — Colours usually differ simultaneously in at least two respects, and the terms above are very convenient in practice, as expressing difference in both tint and tone, when the difference in hue is unimportant. Thus a colour is said to be "paler" when it is poorer in tint, and at the same time lighter in tone; and a colour is said to be "deeper" when it is simultaneously richer in tint and darker in tone — the hue in both cases being pretty constant. We may instance the colours of pale and deep lemon yellow sold by artists' colourmen.

Equivalent Grey. — Every chromatic colour is equivalent in tone to a grey produced by mixing black and white in certain proportions, or in other words, to a white of a certain degree of luminosity.

Primary Colours (see Chap. Two.) are the three colours which are elementary sensations, from the mixture of which all other positive colours can be produced; but which cannot themselves be produced by mixtures of other colours.

Secondary Colours are produced by mixing any two of the primary colours. Thus red and green furnish *orange-red, orange, orange-yellow, yellow* and *yellowish-green,* according to the proportions in which they are mixed. Similarly, red and blue give *violet, purple,* etc. And blue and green yield *bluish-green* and *greenish-blue.*

All these results produced by mixing two of the primary colours in varying proportions, may be termed secondary colours. We have shown in Chapter Two. that richer secondary colours can be excited by simple light than by a mixture of two different kinds of light.

Tertiary Colours have been defined as those produced by mixing any two of the secondary colours. The term is, however, quite unnecessary, and it would be misleading to retain it, for there can be no tertiary colour in a chromatic sense, and this was the old meaning of the term.

By mixing two secondary colours we always produce a certain amount of white; for in any two secondary colours all three primaries are present.

We have, in fact, four cases to consider.

I. *The primaries are in such proportions that all three sets of colour nerves are equally stimulated.* Result — white or grey.

II. *Two sets of nerves are equally stimulated, and the third to a less extent.* Result — tint of a secondary colour.

III. *Two are equally stimulated, and the third to a greater extent* — tint of primary colour.

IV. *All three sets of nerves are stimulated to an unequal extent* — tint of secondary colour.

Broken Colours. — The so-called "broken colours" are colours which are largely mixed with the sensation of blackness. They are, in fact shades of either primary or secondary colours; or of tints of primary or secondary colours.

The primary and secondary colours and their tints, shades and shades of tints, include all possible colours.

The principal broken colours may be classified as follows:

Broken orange-yellow, orange-red, red and purplish red . . .	*The Browns.*
Broken yellow	*Citrine.*
Broken greenish yellow . . .	*Olive.*
Broken green, bluish green, blue, violet, and purple . . .	*The Grays.*

The browns and grays are often called Semi-Neutral Colours.

Warm and Cold Colours. — Artists have originated a distinction between "warm" and "cold" colours. This classification is founded more on association, than on any inherent property of the colours.

Yellow, orange, and red, are the prevailing colours of sunlight and fire, and hence have been termed the warm colours; for an analogous reason colours more or less allied to blue have been called the cold colours.

The colours of ordinary pigments have no perceptible heating effect upon the eye. It can indeed be shown by placing a very delicate thermometer in the prismatic solar spectrum that the heating effect gradually increases from the violet towards the red end. But it has been pointed out by Von Bezold [2] that this is due to the fact that in the spectrum produced by a prism the ether waves are more crowded together at the red end; and that in a *normal* spectrum, which can be produced by diffraction (see treatises on optics), the maximum heating effect occurs in the yellow portion, i.e. corresponds with the maximum of luminosity.

Advancing and Retiring Colours. — Similarly, artists distinguish between *Advancing and Retiring Colours.* White and yellow having the reputation of being the most advancing, and black and blue the most retiring colours. In general colours which are most used for the expression of light have been called advancing, and those most used for the expression of shade retiring.

A partial explanation of the distinction between advancing and retiring colours may be based on the non-achromatism of the human eye. Thus, if we place two surfaces, coloured red and blue respectively, at equal distances from the eye, the red surface will appear the nearer, simply because the red rays are least refracted. And similar results will occur with the intermediate colours of the spectrum.

Local Colour. — By the local colour of an object, we mean its colour when we get close to it, and eliminate all causes tending to interfere with distinct vision. Trees of green local colour often appear purple in the distance. This is an effect of aerial perspective.

Aerial or Colour Perspective refers to the modifications in tint, tone, and in hue which colours undergo when removed to a distance.

The modifications in tone are, to some extent, an effect simply of the distance, and depend on the optical law of inverse squares.

The changes in tint and hue are principally wrought by the action of the atmosphere; and vary according to its thickness, and the amount of water-vapour, smoke, etc., that it contains.

Aerial perspective is as essential to the true representation of colour as linear perspective is to the correct reproduction of form.

The scheme of classification given overleaf will be found useful in collecting some of our definitions.

[1] The distinction between gr*e*y and gr*a*y should be carefully observed. Grey is composed only of black and white; the term gray is applied to any broken colour of a cool hue, and therefore belongs to the class of chromatic colours.

[2] A translation of Von Bezold's "Colour in its Relation to Art and Art Industry," has been published in America (Prang & Co., Boston).

Colour.	Negative.	Black	Achromatic, or Neutral colours.
	Positive.	Grey	
		White	
		The primary and secondary colours, and their tints, shades, and shades of tints . . .	Chromatic colours, or Hues.

Chapter Four - Contrast and Harmony of Colours

Contrast of Colour. — In all the cases we have considered so far there has always been a physical cause for an alteration in the tone, tint, or hue of a colour. Thus we have seen that the colour of an object will vary with the kind and intensity of the illumination, with its power of selective absorption, with its distance from the eye, and with the interposition of atmosphere, vapour, etc. But colours may be changed without any of these conditions being altered, simply by associating them with other colours. The cause of this alteration is not physical, but purely physiological.

The mutual modifications which occur when we place colours in juxtaposition with each other are termed the phenomena of contrast of colour. They are governed by well-defined laws which we shall explain in detail. They all depend on the following general principle:

General Principle of Contrast of Colours

When two dissimilar colours are placed in contiguity, they are always modified in such a way as to increase the dissimilarity.

If they are different in tone (luminosity), then the tone of the brighter colour will be heightened, i.e. it will appear still brighter, and that of the darker one will be lowered. If they are different in optical composition — i.e. in hue, tint (purity or proportion of white light), or both — then they will be mutually modified, so that the difference in optical composition is enhanced.

The phenomena of contrast of colour were first investigated and referred to a definite law by the French chemist Chevreul, some fifty years ago, and his book is even now accepted as the standard — probably because the only — work on the subject.

After careful study of Chevreul we cannot recommend it for the artist's perusal. The inferences Chevreul drew from his fundamental experiment on contrast of tone, are partially false if the experiment is properly performed, and his very definition of "tone" is eminently unsatisfactory, and altogether hopelessly confusing. He makes no distinction between purity and luminosity, and uses the word *"tone"* in both senses. In this chapter we shall attempt to describe the effects more accurately, and to classify them anew. The word *tone* will, as defined in Chapter Three, be used only in the sense of luminosity.

Standard Colour. Before proceeding to study the effects of contrast it will be necessary to consider on what background we shall regard a colour as standard, so that, when we describe it as being modified in a certain way, we mean relatively to its appearance on this background. It is evidently desirable that the background should be such as not to alter it in tone, or in optical composition, and therefore, by the principle just enunciated, it should not differ from it either in tone or optical composition. In fact, we are driven back on the only choice we have, to *place it on a background of its own colour.*

The contrasts of colour fall naturally into three classes.

1. The neutral colours may be contrasted with each other — *Achromatic Contrast.*

2. Hues may be contrasted with each other — *Chromatic Contrast.*

3. Hues may be contrasted with neutral colours — *Contrast of Chromatic with Achromatic Colours.*

I. Achromatic Contrast

Neutral colours, by being contrasted with each other, can be modified only in one way, i.e. in respect of tone.

Thus a grey placed beside white will appear darker, and beside black lighter, than under other conditions. And in general, a neutral colour is lightened in tone by associating it with a darker neutral colour, and darkened in tone by placing it near a lighter one.

Modification in tone is not, as we shall see, confined to neutral colours; but the following law holds good in all cases.

Law of Modification in Tone. — *When two colours of different tones are placed in juxtaposition they experience a mutual modification in virtue of which the lighter colour is lightened in tone, and the darker one darkened in tone.*

Chromatic Contrast

Chromatic colours may be modified by contrast with each other in three different ways: — 1st, in respect of tone; 2nd, in respect of hue, and finally, in respect of tint. As a rule all of these effects co-exist, and two of them are invariably present.

Suppose we place red and blue in juxtaposition. The red will appear more orange in hue, and richer in tint; and the blue will appear more greenish in hue and also richer in tint. With respect to the modifications in tint and hue respectively, examination of all possible cases has enabled us to lay down the following laws.

Law of Modification in Tint. — *A colour always appears richer in tint by associating it with any other colour, except one more saturated in its own hue. It will then appear poorer in tint.*

The amount of change will vary directly with the chromatic difference of the colours, and will also depend on their relative saturation.

Law of Modification in Hue. [1] — *When two dissimilar hues are placed in contiguity they experience a mutual modification, so that each appears as if it has been mixed with the complementary of the other.*

Now, suppose in the case above considered that the blue is dark in tone, and the red comparatively light. It is evident that modification in tone will accompany the modifications in hue and tint. If, however, we mix the blue with white of a lighter tone than the red (this will always be the case with pigments) we can, by adjusting the proportions, obtain a tint of the blue which will be equal in tone to the red, and by placing it beside the red, can then get modification in hue and tint unaccompanied by modification in tone.

Similarly, by juxtaposing two colours of the same hue, we can, if one of them is darker in tone than the other, obtain modification in tone and tint unaccompanied by modification in hue.

It follows, from our third law, that a colour always appears poorest in tint on a background of its own hue, and is richer in tint when associated with any other colour. But the more closely allied the hue of the contrasting colours the less will they enrich each other.

A word should be said about the particular case in which the contrasting colours are *complementary*. Here there is no change in hue; but each colour appears richer in tint than under any other condition. Modification in tone will also occur unless the two colours are equal in luminosity.

Contrast of Chromatic with Achromatic Colours

Here the following effects may occur:

I. Mutual modification in tone. If the neutral colour is black or white this modification must always occur, as black is darker, and white lighter in tone than any other colour. But if the neutral colour be grey, it may happen that it is of the same tone as the chromatic colour with which it is associated, and the modification will not occur.

II. The neutral colour is always more or less tinged with the complementary of the chromatic colour — with white the effect is often scarcely noticeable; but with grey and black is often very pronounced. The chromatic colour is also slightly altered in hue, so as to move towards the more distant part of the Spectrum.

III. The chromatic colour is deepened in tint in all cases.

The contrast of hues with neutral colours is of inestimable use to the artist, and gives a great charm to his colouring. Association with a hue of some sort gives value to neutral colours, and a chromatic effect becomes more precious to us when associated with neutrality.

Harmony of Colour

Colours are said to be harmonised when their arrangement is satisfactory to the eye. Harmony of colour has not yet been reduced to definite laws; but there are certain principles in connection with it which seem to be pretty generally recognised.

Colours which are chromatically closely related to one another, such as green and yellow, are discordant when they are arranged so that there is an *abrupt transition* from one to the other. Such colours are, as we have already seen, almost at their dullest when juxtaposed.

In nature, however, some of the most beautiful effects of colour are produced by what is called the *Small Interval;* for example, the combination of green and greenish-yellow in sunlit foliage, and of blue and green when the sky is seen through trees. But we find that in nature the colours are never allowed to come in contact; but are harmonised either by being separated by neutral colours, or by being imperceptibly gradated and blended into each other.

Gradation of colour in nature is universal. Ruskin says in his "Elements of Drawing:" "The preciousness and pleasantness of colour depends more on this than on any other of its qualities, for gradation is to colours just what curvature is to lines. The difference in mere beauty between a gradated and ungradated colour may be seen by laying an even tint of rose-colour on paper and putting a rose-leaf beside it."

Colours which are, chromatically, comparatively far apart, form arrangements which are more or less satisfactory.

With complementary colours which are at all saturated the contrast is so excessive that a harsh effect is sometimes apt to be produced. The combinations of complementary colours are principally valuable when it is desired to give effect and brilliancy to rather dull colours.

Balance of Colour. — It has been stated by some writers that the most perfect harmony is produced when the colours are in such proportions that, by their admixture white or grey would be produced; and certain numbers have been assigned to the various colours such that, if the areas of the colours in a composition are proportional to these numbers, the best effect will be produced.

This is, however, all nonsense, although there may be some ground for the supposition that for perfect harmony it is necessary that all three colour sensations should be called into action. The above writers have assumed that harmony depends on the balance of colour sensations. As a matter of fact we find, by examining the masterpieces of the most renowned colourists, that the connection does not hold good. There is invariably a dominant colour.

Harmony of colour depends rather on aesthetic than on optical balance. It is entirely a question of feeling, and cannot be reduced to rules.

In conclusion, it may be stated that the effects of harmony in painting, as "in music, are increased by the occasional introduction of discords.

[1] Chevreul, in his classification of the phenomena of contrast, recognised only two possible modifications, which he termed "contrast of tone" and "contrast of colour." We have shown elsewhere that there are three modifications which have to be considered.

Part Two - On Pigments Generally

Chapter Five - The Origin and Classification of Pigments

A Pigment is a powdered substance used for the representation of colour. A pigment mixed with a medium constitutes a *paint.*

It will be seen from our introduction that the pigments employed by the ancient painters were mainly derived from native earths. These substances had already seen the wear and tear of centuries, and were hence extremely permanent. A certain amount of mechanical preparation was necessary to fit them for use, and this was, until modern times, performed by the artist in his studio.

The birth of Chemistry in the last century gave a new departure to the history of pigments. With the progress of chemical science artificial preparations were gradually discovered, and the function of the colour-maker sprang into existence. At the present time our most important pigments are, almost without exception, artificial compounds. Colour-making is an important branch of industry, and has been so specialised that some firms restrict themselves to the manufacture of a particular pigment, in the production of which they are often *facile princeps,* and enjoy in consequence a continental reputation.

Skilful colour-making requires great experience in the mechanical habitudes of matter, as well as a certain amount of chemical knowledge. The mere chemist is' often forcibly reminded that between the analysis of a pigment and its successful production there is a great gulf fixed. As Mr. Haweis remarks, in speaking of old violins, "In the perfection of every technical trade there is something which defies analysis." A Stradivarius violin, however carefully taken to pieces, will not betray the secrets of its manufacture; nor will, in many cases, the analysis of a pigment afford much clue to its synthesis.

Many of our best pigments are prepared by processes which are very jealously guarded by the colour-makers. In Part Three of this book, the artist will be told all that is known, outside manufacturing circles, of the constitution of his pigments.

Pigments are obtained from the mineral, animal, and vegetable kingdoms, and thus we may classify them broadly into three divisions.

Pigments Obtained from the Mineral Kingdom

I. Native Pigments. — This class comprises *Genuine Ultramarine,* the *Ochres, Umbers, Siennas* and other native earths. These claim attention on account of their great durability, and also because they were the substances which were first employed in painting. They require no preparation except washing, grinding, and, in some cases, calcining; and as a rule are rather dull, but very useful pigments. They are excelled in most respects by those mineral pigments which are prepared by chemical processes. The native brown pigments are, however, superior to any artificial preparations.

II. Artificial Pigments. — These are prepared either by the action of heat on the proper ingredients, or by precipitation from aqueous solutions. In other words, they are made either by wet or dry processes.

1. Pigments made by the dry process comprise the *Vermilions, Cadmiums,* and *Mars Colours, Artificial Ultramarine, Cobalt, Smalt, Venetian Red,* etc. These are, as a rule, more permanent than the pigments obtained in the wet way.

2. Pigments made by the wet process: such as *Aureolin, Chrome Yellows, Lemon Yellow, Pure Scarlet, Emerald Green, White Lead,* etc. The particles of these pigments are often more or less crystalline in structure.

Sometimes a pigment can be made either by wet or dry processes. In this case the latter method will generally be preferable, as giving the more durable product.

Pigments Obtained from the Animal Kingdom

Of all the members of the animal kingdom the cochineal insect makes the best contribution to the palette; furnishing us with *Carmine* and *Crimson, Scarlet,* and *Purple Lakes.*

Indian Yellow, or euxanthate of magnesium, is obtained from the urine of the camel.

Gallstone is derived from a calculus which is formed in the gall-bladders of oxen.

Sepia is obtained from a secretion of the *Sepia officinalis,* a cuttle fish.

Prussian Blue may be regarded as indirectly derived from the animal kingdom, inasmuch as the prussiate of potash used in its manufacture is obtained by fusing refuse animal matter with impure potassium carbonate.

Pigments Obtained from the Vegetable Kingdom

These for the most part are Lakes.

A Lake is a pigment prepared by precipitating an animal or vegetable colouring matter in combination with a metallic base, usually alumina.

A Carmine. — When two or more lakes of different strengths are prepared from the same colouring matter, that lake which contains the greatest proportion of colouring matter to metallic oxide is termed a *Carmine* — as, for instance, *Cochineal Carmine* (or Carmine *par excellence*), *Madder Carmine, Violet Carmine,* etc.

A Pink. — Some lakes are rather anomalously called 'pinks,' e.g. *Italian Pink* and *Brown Pink.*

It has been shown that many vegetable colouring matters exist in the plants, as glucosides, i.e. they are bodies which may be decomposed by chemical re-agents, or by a natural process of fermentation, into *glucose* and a *colouring principle.*

Indigo is obtained from the leaves of the *Indigo fera* plant, and is formed by fermentation from the glucoside *Indican.*

Madder Lakes are prepared from the madder root, which contains the glucoside *rubian.*

Brown Pink is obtained from Persian and Avignon berries — glucoside *rhamnin.*

Yellow Lake and *Italian Pink* are obtained from quercitron bark — glucoside *quercitrin.*

Olive Lake is made from the green ebony or laburnum.

Indian Lake and *Gamboge* are prepared from resinous secretions.

Among the foregoing pigments the Madder Lakes stand out conspicuously for beauty of colour and permanence.

Blue Black, the charcoal of the vine stalk, and *Lamp Black,* the soot obtained by burning resinous substances, must also be classed with the pigments of vegetable origin.

Chapter Six - The General Properties of Pigments

THE general properties of pigments may be classified as follows:—

Colour	Physical properties.
Transparency	
Opacity	
Specific Gravity	
Working property	
Fineness of Texture	
Body	
Crispness and Setting-up	
Drying power	Chemical properties.
Permanence	

The possession of the last property — that of permanence — should be regarded as a *sine quâ non*. Without it all other qualifications put together are of no esteem with the artist who values his reputation. We shall therefore give it a distinct consideration in the next chapter.

Colour. — We have already explained the colours of pigments under the heading "Colours of Natural Bodies," and have seen that in general each particle of a pigment may be regarded as a small transparent body which colours light by selective absorption. It is not at all difficult to conceive that the most opaque pigment may be composed of transparent particles. A cloud is opaque, although we know that its structural elements are transparent globules of water, and a piece of paper will be seen under the microscope to consist of transparent fibres. Vermilion — one of our most opaque pigments — occurs in nature in transparent crystals.

Effect of Immersing a Pigment in a Medium. — A chromatically coloured pigment when immersed in water gains in richness of colour, but loses luminosity. The effect is to reduce the quantity of white light which is reflected from the exterior surfaces of the particles. This reflection of white light depends upon the rupture of optical continuity caused by light passing from the air into the much denser particles of pigment. When the light passes from water into the particles of pigment, there is not nearly so much difference of density, and consequently not nearly as much reflection of white light. The chromatically coloured light is of course due to reflections from the *interior* surfaces of the particles after absorption has taken place. In oil, which is more refractive than water, the above effects are still further emphasized.

Value of Oil as a Medium. — It will be seen from the above explanation that much richer effects are possible in oil than in water, and also greater transparency. Furthermore the effects of the oil medium *persist,* for a dry film of oil is just as refractive as ever; while in water-colour they vanish on drying.

Value of Water as a Medium. — Water-colour is especially suitable for delicacy of colouring and for the expression of atmosphere.

Result of Increasing the Thickness of a Pigment. — We have shown, in Chapter One, that the colour of pigments is due to the fact that they are transparent to certain waves of light, and opaque to others. But there is in nature no such thing as absolute transparency for any kind of ray. Chromatically coloured bodies are in fact only *more* transparent to some rays than to others, and hence with increase of thickness we get decreased luminosity, and also, to some extent, change of hue. Thus a thin wash of carmine is pink; a thick wash much darker in tone and more scarlet in hue.

Beauty of Colour. — A pigment may possess beauty of colour in two ways. It may be delicate, pure, and brilliant; or it may be deep, rich, and intense. In the production of pigments, delicacy and depth of colour are found to be antagonistic qualities, which cannot co-exist to any great extent. Perfect success in producing one of them is always attended with more or less of failure with respect to the other, and when they are united it is with some sacrifice of both. Hence it is well to provide for the palette two pigments of each colour, one eminent for delicate beauty, the other for richness and depth.

Transparency, the property which enables us to see through a pigment, is essential in glazing, and adds greatly to the value of those pigments which are used for the expression of shade.

Opacity is the opposite of transparency, and characterises pigments which are used for the expression of light. As excellencies, therefore, transparency and opacity are only relative.

With regard to transparent and opaque pigments generally, it is worthy of attention that in the practice of the oil-painter, the best effects of the -former are produced when they are used with a resinous varnish, and of the latter in oil; and that the two become united with best effect in a mixture of these vehicles.

Specific Gravity. — Pigments vary very much in this respect. The specific gravities of some of the heavier inorganic pigments are given below: —

Red lead	9·1
Vermilion	8·2
White lead	6·5
Pure Scarlet	6·2
Chrome yellow . . .	5·7
Zinc white	5·6
Cadmium yellow . . .	4·8

It will be seen, from the above list, that there is a distinct connection between high Specific Gravity and Opacity.

Working Property depends chiefly upon fineness of texture, and what is called *body* in pigments; yet every pigment has its peculiarities of working, both in water and oil, and these must become the matter of every artist's personal experience. Some of the best pigments are the most difficult of management, while many ineligible pigments are rich in body and free in working.

Fineness of Texture is produced chiefly by careful grinding and levigation.

Body. — This term is often used synonymously with opacity or power of obliterating a surface; but properly means *tingeing* power. We may compare the body of two samples of a pigment — say, chrome yellow, by mixing equal weights of them with equal, and relatively large, weights of white lead.

Crispness and Setting-up. — These qualities, which enable a pigment to keep its place on the canvas, are contrary to the nature of many pigments, and can only be conferred by painting them with a megilp or gelatinous vehicle. Glazing can only be performed with a vehicle which keeps its place, or with pigments which confer this property on the vehicle, as some lakes and transparent pigments do.

Drying Power. — The drying of an oil is a chemical process attended with absorption of oxygen from the atmosphere. Pigments may facilitate or retard this process. In the latter case the artist has recourse to *dryers.*

With light colours — *sugar of lead, litharge,* and *sulphate of zinc,* either finely ground or in solution in oil, are used; and for lakes, *japanners' gold size,* and *boiled oil. Manganese* and *verdigris* are often employed with the darker colours.

It would be well if lead and copper could be altogether banished from the list of siccatives. No artist with any regard for the permanence of his work should employ them except in extreme cases, and then only in the smallest possible quantity. Sulphate of zinc, as a siccative, is less powerful than sugar of lead; but, in a chemical sense, is far preferable.

The state of the atmosphere has a strong influence on the drying of pigments, and the direct rays of the sun are powerfully active in rendering oils siccative. This mode of drying was probably resorted to in the warm climate of Italy before dryers were discovered. Accidental circumstances may also retard drying, and among these none is to be more guarded against by the artist than the presence of soap and alkali, too often left in the washing of his brushes. To avoid this, brushes should always be carefully cleansed with linseed oil and turpentine.

To the other desirable attributes of pigments it would be well if we could in all cases add the property of being *innocuous.* As, however, this cannot be, and pigments are by no means to be sacrificed because they are poisonous, it would be well if artists would pay strict attention to cleanliness, and avoid the practice, so common in water-colour painting, of putting the brush in the mouth.

Chapter Seven - The Permanence of Pigments

As colour itself is relative, so is durability of colour relative. No pigment is so permanent that nothing will alter its colour, and, on the other hand, no pigment is so fugitive that it will not last under favouring conditions.

The colour of *Genuine Ultramarine,* which will endure for centuries under ordinary circumstances, maybe at once destroyed by a drop of lemon juice; and the generally fugitive *Carmine* will, when secluded from light and air, last fifty years or more.

Again, there have been works of art in which the white of lead has retained its freshness for ages in a pure atmosphere, but has been blackened by a few hours' exposure to foul air.

It is therefore durability under the ordinary conditions of painting which entitles a pigment to the character of permanence.

The Chemistry of Permanence. — Chemical change is, in all cases, the cause of want of permanence among pigments. This chemical change may, under the ordinary conditions of painting, be effected in the following ways:

(1.) *By the Action of Light.*

(2.) *By the Action of the Atmosphere.*

(3.) *By the Action of the Medium.*

(4.) *By the Mutual Action of Pigments which have been mixed together.*

I.— Action of Light.

Light acts principally on the pigments of organic origin, and on the more unstable of the inorganic pigments. The vibrations communicated by ether waves (especially the rapid vibration due to the rays at the violet end of the spectrum) seem to be able to shatter up molecules which are complex in structure, or which are not held together by strong chemical affinity. Light, even when it is not itself able to effect the decomposition of a pigment, greatly facilitates its decomposition by other agencies. The action of light is much more marked in water-colour than in oil, owing to the thinness of the film of colour. A list of the pigments affected by light will be found in the Appendix.

II.— Action of the Atmosphere.

The normal atmosphere consists of a mixture of *oxygen* and *nitrogen* gases in the proportion of four volumes of the latter to one of the former. A small but fairly constant quantity of *carbonic acid* (.04 per cent.) is also present, and a certain amount of *water vapour,* which varies immensely with the temperature.

The atmosphere of towns generally contains small quantities of *sulphurous* and *sulphuric acids,* derived from the combustion of coal, and is often contaminated with *sulphuretted hydrogen.* The presence of this last gas, which is due to exhalations from sewers, gas works, etc., possesses, as we shall see, a special significance for the artist.

The action of the nitrogen and carbonic acid of the atmosphere may be at once dismissed as practically *nil.*

Action of Atmospheric Oxygen. — Oxygen is powerfully active as an oxidizing agent, especially in the allotropic condition known as "ozone," and when assisted by sunlight and moisture. Oil paintings are far less liable than water colours to atmospheric action. It has indeed been assumed that pigments when locked up in oils and varnishes are safe from all possibility of change from such causes; but from what we know of the diffusion of gases through membranes we must hesitate to describe these films of oil and varnish as absolutely impervious.

Water-colour paintings are particularly liable to the action of atmospheric oxygen, and, as is well known, certain pigments will in water fade rapidly from this cause, which in oil are comparatively stable.

Action of Atmospheric Moisture. — The moisture present in the atmosphere will take a long time to have any appreciable action on the front of a well-varnished oil painting. But in water-colour painting we have absolutely no protection against its influence. It probably renders powerful assistance to oxidation by softening the thin film of gum, and bringing the oxygen into closer relation with the particles of pigment. An actual deposit of water on a picture will especially facilitate oxidation, for water dissolves twice as much oxygen as nitrogen.

It should be noted that oil paintings are usually most liable to the attacks of atmospheric moisture, etc., through the *back* of the canvas.

Action of Sulphuretted Hydrogen. — Sulphuretted hydrogen forms with some metals dark coloured sulphides of great stability, and consequently pigments which have these metals as bases are liable, if exposed to its influence, to be more or less discoloured. Unfortunately, sulphuretted hydrogen singles out white lead, our most useful oil-colour, for special attack.

Sulphuretted hydrogen in the atmosphere gets slowly oxidized to sulphurous, and thence to sulphuric acid. But the combustion of coal and gas is the principal source of the sulphur acids in the atmosphere. These sulphur acids must, if present in appreciable quantity, have a very injurious effect on pictures. Fortunately they are readily removed by a good shower of rain.

It has been stated that the destruction of the bindings of books in libraries lighted by gas is due to the slow action of sulphuric acid derived from its combustion. The employment of electric light in picture galleries, recommended in Chapter L from purely optical considerations, is thus doubly advantageous.

The facility with which pigments bear exposure to light and to atmospheric oxygen and moisture should be regarded as the principal test of their permanence. A picture *may* meet with sulphuretted hydrogen, but *must* be exposed to light and atmosphere.

III.— Action of the Medium

(1.) **In Oil-colour.** — Oil in drying absorbs oxygen in considerable quantity. This is usually obtained from the atmosphere, but sometimes may be taken from a pigment, if the latter is at all reducible. Thus it is that the chromates are apt to turn green in oil.

When oils have been boiled with oxide of lead, manganese, or zinc, or when some of the *pot pourris* called *megilps* are used, the chemistry of the subject is much more complicated, and in many cases permanence is sacrificed in order to secure rapid dessication. Many mediums have been justly blamed for their injurious effects upon pigments. The most permanent pigment may be ruined by employing it with an untrustworthy vehicle.

(2.) **In Water-colour.** — Here water-colour has for once the advantage; for the drying of a water medium is simply a question of evaporation, and solidification of dissolved gum, and no chemical change takes place.

IV.— Action of Pigments on Each Other

Two solid substances cannot act on each other chemically. For two bodies to have a chemical action on each other it is necessary that one of them should be in the liquid or gaseous state. However much we may mix and grind two pigments together, the particles of each are readily discernible under the microscope. The molecules cannot thus be brought into chemical relation, and the state of affairs undergoes no change by immersing our two pigments in a medium *provided that they are absolutely insoluble in that medium.* If, however, one or both be soluble, then the ultimate molecules are brought into contact, and chemical action is favoured. Here we see the importance of *insolubility* as a qualification of a pigment.

It is probable, however, that few pigments are absolutely insoluble in the mediums with which they are employed, and so *in most cases mixture of pigments is unfavourable to permanence.* The painter who values his picture will therefore make his mixtures as simple as possible.

As chemical action is greatly favoured by thoroughness of mixture, it is evidently a bad plan to *grind* pigments with each other. Many of the peculiarities of the Flemish School of Painting may be attributed to the practice of grinding pigments together instead of blending them on the palette. The method has now fallen into disuse, and in many cases undoubtedly conduces to dinginess of colour.

There is usually a broad kind of chemical relationship between a solvent and the substance it dissolves. Thus inorganic substances, as a rule, dissolve best in water, while organic bodies are most soluble in alcohol, oil, turpentine, etc. Most of our pigments are inorganic, and many of these are slightly soluble in water, although absolutely insoluble in oil, or in a mixture of oil and turpentine. Here again we see that the oil medium has a distinct advantage.

Turpentine, by reason of its greater fluidity, is inferior to oil as a means of isolating particles of pigment, and hence it is probably advisable to employ it in as small proportion as possible.

There are two methods of practice which prevail among artists. The first method is to use as few pigments as possible, and rely principally upon admixture. The second is to have as many pigments as possible.

Although it is possible for the artist to multiply his pigments unnecessarily, yet there is no doubt that the second plan is in principle far preferable. Not only are the mixtures often less permanent, but they are never so bright in colour as the original pigments. We have shown in Chapter Two that, whenever we mix pigments together, more or less black is always produced in consequence of absorption.

Cadmium orange, which is naturally an orange pigment, and not composed of a mixture of red and yellow particles, is preferable to many mixtures of red and yellow pigments in a chemical sense, and to all such mixtures in an artistic sense.

The artist would require a considerable knowledge of chemistry to be able to predict the permanence of any particular mixture of pigments, and the number of common mixtures is so large that it would be impossible in a work like the present to investigate their stability in detail. There are, however, two classes of pigments — those with *lead* and *iron* bases respectively — which are particularly noted for often having a strong action on other colours with which they are mixed. The pigments which thus suffer are enumerated in the Appendix. An ivory or horn palette knife should always be used with those which are acted on by iron and, indeed, is always preferable.

Dilution of Pigments. — In most of the cases we have considered, the chemical action will be favoured by diluting the pigment. This dilution may be effected in three ways: —

(1.) By a too free use of the vehicle.

(2.) By spreading a small quantity of pigment over a relatively large surface.

(3.) By mixing it with other pigments.

This last method of dilution enforces the expediency of mixing pigments together as little as possible, quite apart from any consideration of their chemical action on each other.

Effect of Time. — In all the methods of chemical decomposition we have described, *time* plays a very important part in the process.

It has been observed that time, of long or short duration, often has on a pigment the effect of heat, more or less intense; and that the action of time upon a pigment may often be predicted from the action of heat. This statement, founded purely on practical observation, seems to have a definite basis in theory, for, according to the doctrine of conservation of energy, the rays of light absorbed by substances are converted into heat.

It has sometimes been imagined that pigments which have been vitrified by intense heat are, when ground in oil or water, the most durable to be had. If this were the case the artist could not do better than furnish his palette with a supply of well-burnt and levigated enamel pigments. But although such pigments stand well when fluxed on glass, or in enamel, they are almost without exception subject to the most serious changes when ground to the degree of fineness necessary for their use as pigments.

Enamel and Fresco Painting. — Those pigments which will withstand the action of strong heat are eligible for enamel painting, and those which are unaffected by lime can be used in fresco. Lists of these pigments will be found in the Appendix.

Part Three - On Pigments Individually

Chapter Eight - White Pigments

THE oil painter is not particularly well furnished with white pigments. A thoroughly unexceptionable white pigment, combining the opacity and body of white lead with the permanence of zinc white, is still a desideratum.

In water-colour the state of things is more satisfactory. Chinese white is unexceptionable in respect of body and permanence; but is rather wanting in opacity.

Lead Whites

The principal lead whites used by artists are *Flake White, Cremnitz White,* and *Blanc d'Argent.* These are all carbonates of lead, and invariably contain a small percentage of hydrated oxide of lead.

Pure carbonate of lead does not make a good paint. It is opaque and beautifully white; but has no great body (covering power). [1] It also dries rather slowly, and is apt to separate from the oil.

The presence of the hydrated oxide greatly increases the value of the pigment. It combines chemically with the oil to form an elastic, rapidly drying varnish, and by being in intimate combination both with oil and carbonate of lead, it not only enables a given weight of pigment to cover a larger area, but also prevents any possibility of subsidence. At the same time, however, the paint is decreased in opacity.

It will thus be seen that with certain proportions of lead carbonate and hydrated oxide, the artistic efficiency of white lead will be at a maximum: i.e. the best combination of body, opacity, and drying power will be produced. Our principal authorities seem to agree that the proportion of hydrated oxide should be about 25 per cent.

In point of colour and body the white leads are superior to all other whites. The great drawback to their employment is their tendency to blacken under the influence of sulphuretted hydrogen, and this gas is, unfortunately, almost invariably present in the atmosphere. In oil and varnish they dry well without assistance, and are comparatively durable; the medium in drying forms a protective film which greatly retards the action of foul air; but in water, distemper, fresco, or crayon, they should not be employed.

White leads are found in course of time to lose a portion of their opacity. If over some dry oil-colour rubs, we brush just enough white lead to completely obscure them, it will be found, after a time, that the forms and colours of the rubs are indistinctly visible. The result is probably due to gradual saponification.

It has been shown that white lead is less liable to be affected by sulphuretted hydrogen when the pictures in which it is employed are exposed to strong light; and that, when it has been tarnished, exposure to strong light will restore the colour.

This effect is a result of oxidation; the black sulphide of lead is oxidized to sulphate of lead, which is white.

Water-colour drawings in which the white lead has gone black, may be restored by treating them with a solution of peroxide of hydrogen. This powerful oxidizing agent rapidly converts the black sulphide into white sulphate.

White lead cannot be safely mixed with vegetable lakes, even with those of madder, or with gamboge; but with most other colours it may be safely compounded.

In oil-painting, white lead is essential in the ground, in dead colouring, in the formation of tints, and in scumbling. In fact it is more extensively used than any other pigment. It is very poisonous.

It should be observed that the descriptions below give the original distinctions. There is now so little difference between the best white leads, that it is usual for artists' colourmen to sell the same article under all three names.

Flake White

Called, when levigated, *Body White*, is an English white lead. It has the best body of all white leads.

Cremnitz White

Or *Crems White*, is manufactured at Kremnitz in Hungary. It is the whitest of all the white-leads; but is inferior in body to flake white.

Blanc D'argent

Is a French variety. It has less body than flake white; but is sometimes preferred by artists for its exquisite colour.

Zinc White

Is either the anhydrous oxide, the hydrated oxide, or the hydrated basic carbonate of zinc. It varies in opacity and colour according to the mode of manufacture; but may always be relied upon for permanence. In opacity it does not approach white lead; but it is never tarnished by sulphuretted hydrogen. It might perhaps be advantageously glazed over white lead, and also be used as a medium of interposition between white lead and those colours which are injured by it, such as crimson lake, gamboge, etc.

When skilfully prepared, the colour and body of zinc white are sufficient to qualify it for general use as an oil-colour. In water it has been superseded by Chinese white. It does not dry so rapidly as white lead; but possesses the advantage of being perfectly innocuous.

Chinese White

The introduction, in 1834, of this peculiar preparation of oxide of zinc has proved an incalculable boon to water-colour painters, who formerly had no white which combined perfect permanence with good body in working. Its invention obviated the necessity of using white lead, a pigment which, though it may be employed with comparative safety in oil, is quite unfitted for water. Since the period of its introduction, Chinese white has been generally preferred by water-colour artists, as being the most eligible in their peculiar department. Previous to that period the complaints of whites changing were of constant occurrence; but in no instance has any picture, in which this white has been used, suffered from its employment.

Chinese white, when properly prepared, works and washes well, possesses no pasty or clogging properties, and is beautifully white. Moreover, it has the desirable quality of dense body; so much so, that, as the painter works, his effects remain unaltered by the drying of the colour. It may also be safely blended with other pigments.

Without the artistic drawbacks of permanent white, or the chemical defects of white lead, and possessing the advantages of both of these pigments, Chinese white cannot but be considered a most important acquisition.

It is a matter of regret that this pigment is not equally efficacious in oil.

Permanent White

Also called *Constant White,* is sulphate of barium, and is, when well prepared, a fair water-colour pigment. In oil it has less opacity. It works in a somewhat unpleasant and unsatisfactory way, and is considerably lower in tone when wet than when dry. This fault subjects even an experienced artist to great uncertainty when he uses it in compound tints. The semi-transparency of the white, while wet, prevents his judging of the true tint until his colour has dried.

This white is, as its name implies, perfectly permanent, and is quite innocuous.

[1] The term "covering power" is rather vague. It may mean: (1) power of obliterating an under surface, or (2) power of stretching over a surface. In the first sense it is synonymous with opacity; in the second with body, and in this latter sense is used above.

Chapter Nine - Red Pigments

OUR red pigments, both in water and oil, leave little to be desired. The Madder Lakes are permanent and transparent, and the Vermilions permanent and opaque. A permanent and transparent scarlet would however be a great acquisition.

The Vermilions

Vermilion is sulphide of mercury, and occurs native as *Cinnabar* in California, Peru, Spain and China. Cinnabar, when carefully ground and levigated, formed a pigment which was highly esteemed by ancient painters. On account of its scarcity it was very valuable, and among the Romans its price was fixed by the State.

The vermilions of the present day, however, are all artificial compounds; native vermilion is commercially obsolete.

Vermilion can be made both by wet and dry processes. Perhaps the most brilliant ones are produced in the wet way; but the dry process is almost exclusively adopted, and probably yields the most permanent products.

The vermilions of commerce are either European or Chinese. The former usually incline to orange and the latter to crimson.

Vermilion

Is prepared either of a deep or pale colour. When pure and well-made it is one of our most permanent pigments, being entirely unaffected by light, time or foul air. It is eligible in either oil, water, or fresco; but cannot be used in enamel, as it is volatile at a red heat.

Vermilion possesses great body, weight and opacity; it is a somewhat slow dryer, and does not, when dry, retain that brilliancy which is peculiar to it in the wet state.

The best vermilions are of a powerful vivid colour, and more brilliant than all other reds except the scarlet iodide of mercury. As far as its own colour is concerned, vermilion may safely be compounded with other pigments; but its heaviness renders it liable to separate from its compounds, hence it mixes best with the heavier colours. Its great opacity and habit of washing up render it difficult to manage. Skilfully used it is a very serviceable colour.

Scarlet Vermilion

Only differs from the preceding in being more scarlet in hue, and washing better. At one time the Dutch alone possessed the secret of giving to vermilion a rich scarlet colour.

Extract of Vermilion

Is identical with scarlet vermilion.

Chinese Vermilion

Or *Carmine Vermilion,* inclines to crimson, and is useful, when mixed with white, for painting the rose tints of delicate complexions. The artist should not attempt to still further modify the hue by mixture with cochineal lakes; for these colours cannot safely be brought in contact with vermilion, either compounded, or as a glaze. If desirable to alter the hue, the madder reds should be employed.

Orange Vermilion

Is rather more transparent than ordinary vermilion, with a clear but not bright orange hue. It also washes better, and for landscape purposes is more generally useful. It affords delicate carnation tints similar to those of Titian and Rubens, and may be employed with excellent results in the scumbling of flesh.

Field's Orange Vermilion

Is a superior preparation to the preceding, being brighter, purer, and clearer. It possesses, also, less opacity, and is not a compound. Both of these pigments are rather reds with an orange hue than strictly orange colours, and we have therefore described them with the reds.

Pure Scarlet

Is iodide of mercury. It has all the body and opacity of vermilion, and is as much inferior to it in permanence as it is superior in brilliancy. Of all artistic pigments it is at once the most dazzling and fugitive, and should have no place on the palette. It can only be used with an ivory palette knife, as iron and most other metals change it to colours varying from yellow to black. It cannot be compounded with other metallic pigments without being utterly destroyed. It is rapidly blackened by sulphuretted hydrogen, and fades altogether when exposed to light and air. In water-colour, a thick glaze of gum arabic or gamboge adds to its stability. As a landscape pigment, it is out of the general scale of nature; but in flower-painting its charms are almost irresistible. Certainly nothing can approach it as a colour for scarlet geraniums; but its beauty is almost as fleeting as the flowers.

Red Chrome

Or *Scarlet Chrome,* is a basic chromate of lead, i.e. a compound of chromate of lead with lead oxide. It is a good dryer, but, like all the lead colours, is blackened by sulphuretted hydrogen.

Mars Red

Or *Rouge de Mars,* is an artificial iron ochre, similar in subdued tint and permanence to the native earths. It is, however, more powerful in its chemical action, and therefore requires to be employed very cautiously with pigments affected by iron.

Mars red possesses all the richness and depth of Indian red with the russet orange hue of light red. Its pale washes are marked by considerable clearness. It is very permanent.

Light Red

Is an ochre of an orange russet hue, and is chiefly valued for its tints. It is prepared by calcining Oxford ochre, and the finer the quality of the ochre, the better will be the resulting red, and the better flesh tints will it yield with white.

Light red has all the good qualities which are common to ochres, it dries capitally, and furnishes an excellent crayon. It is much used both in landscape and figure painting, giving fine grays with cobalt, and serviceable compounds with most other pigments. It is perfectly permanent.

Venetian Red

Is sesquioxide of iron, and is prepared by calcining proto-sulphate of iron. It is similar to light red; but is more powerful and redder in hue. It is very permanent; but, like Mars red, should be cautiously employed with pigments that are affected by iron.

Indian Red

Once called *Persian Red,* is brought from Bengal. It is a natural earth, rich in peroxide of iron. It is of a purple russet hue, of good body, and is valued when of fine quality for the clearness and soft lakey character of its tints. It is very permanent, and a good dryer; but being opaque, and keeping its place badly, it cannot be employed in glazing.

Red Ochre

Is a native earth. It is not so pure in colour, or clear in its tints, as light red.

Red ochre is one of the most ancient pigments, and is, like all the ochres, perfectly permanent.

Cochineal Lakes

These consist of the colouring matter of the cochineal insect precipitated upon an aluminous base. The cochineal insect, or *"coccus cacti"* is a native of Mexico, and is found on a species of cactus, from the juice of which it derives its nourishment. The females, of which there are from one hundred and fifty to two hundred for each male, are marked by the absence of wings, and constitute the commercial article. They are killed by drying in the sun.

The colouring matter of the cochineal insect is not in a free state; but exists in the form of a glucoside called *carminic acid.* By the action of acids, carminic acid may be split up into carmine red and glucose.

Carmine

Is that preparation of cochineal which contains the most colouring matter, and the least aluminous base. Hence it is the richest, deepest, and most intense of the cochineal lakes; but is probably not, as usually stated, the most permanent. Although not to be classed among the permanent pigments, yet carmine is fairly stable under favourable conditions. When pure, well made, and employed alone, it will last for years, especially if protected by oil and varnish. In tint with white lead it will not stand; and, in glazing though little affected by impure air, it is soon discoloured and destroyed by the action of light. It has great power in its full touches, possesses considerable clearness in the pale washes, and works admirably.

In landscape carmine is seldom employed, the colour being chiefly valued for flower-painting and illumination.

Crimson Lake

Is a cochineal lake containing more aluminous base than carmine, and is consequently weaker in colour. Crimson lake possesses a characteristic bloom which is not observable in carmine, and it sometimes stated to be less stable, although this is questionable. It is, however, more generally useful.

Crimson lake is of great service in giving richness to mixed tints; and, like all cochineal colours, is of greater utility in water than in oil. Like all the cochineal pigments it is affected by strong light, and ultimately decolourized. It is a bad dryer.

Scarlet Lake

Is crimson lake with a scarlet hue imparted to it by mixture with vermilion. It has all the properties of crimson lake; but is not so permanent, as vermilion has a destructive action on cochineal lakes. It should never be employed in glazing. In some of the pictures by old masters, the shadows of red objects have entirely disappeared, in consequence of being put in with lake over vermilion.

Madder Lakes

Are prepared by precipitating the colouring matter of the root of the madder plant upon a base of alumina. The madder plant, *"rubia tinctorum"* is largely grown in France and Holland, and the bulk of the English supply is obtained from these countries.

Madder roots are also imported from the Levant, and form the "Turkey Madder" of commerce.

The principal colouring matter obtained from madder is called *Alizarin,* It has a very great interest for chemists, inasmuch as a compound resembling it in all respects has been prepared from Anthracene, one of the coal tar hydrocarbons.

The most careful researches tend to show that fresh madder roots do not contain any appreciable quantity of alizarin; but that they contain a large amount of a glucoside called *Rubian.* The roots, on keeping, undergo a process of fermentation, and the rubian is decomposed by the ferment into alizarin and glucose.

Madder Carmine

Like the carmine of cochineal, is the richest and deepest lake prepared, containing the maximum colouring matter, and the minimum base. It is the only durable carmine for painting, either in water or in oil. In common with the other reds of madder, its faint washes possess greater clearness than those of cochineal; but madder carmine is chiefly valued by the water-colour artist for its deep touches. Its washes are surpassed by those of rose madder.

Rose Madder

This variety is less intense than the preceding, and without its carmine hue. It is of a rich rose colour — a true rose — tending neither to crimson nor scarlet. Marked by a peculiar softness, and an unusual clearness in its pale washes, rose madder affords the most perfect carnation tints known. It is, as indicated above, chiefly valued for its wash. Not liable to change by the action of light, or impure air, it resembles all madder lakes in these respects. Like them, too, it is a tardy dryer in oil, and does not work in water with the entire fulness and facility of the cochineal pigments, and so, when permanence is of no consideration, the latter may still be preferred. Rose madder was used by the old masters, and has apparently undergone no change.

Pink Madder

Was originally a weaker preparation of the preceding; but this is now obsolete. What is now called pink madder is identical with rose madder-

Madder Lake

Is another synonym for rose madder. As some artists know a pigment by one name, and some by another, it has been necessary in trade catalogues to give two or three names to one and the same pigment.

Indian Lake

Or *Lac Lake,* is obtained from the *lac,* or *lacca* of India, a resinous secretion found on the branches of certain plants in Siam, Assam, and Bengal.

Indian lake is rich, transparent, and deep. It is more durable, though less brilliant, than the cochineal colours; but is inferior in both respects to those of madder. Used thickly or in strong glazing, it is of great body and much permanence; but in thin glazing, and in tint with white lead, is decidedly fugitive.

In the properties of drying, etc., it resembles other lakes.

Lac appears to be the lake which has stood best in old pictures. It was probably employed by the Venetians, who had the trade of India when painting flourished at Venice.

Dragons' Blood

Is a resin brought from the East Indies. It is of a warm, semi-transparent, but rather dull red colour; which is deepened by impure air, and darkened by light.

White lead soon destroys it, and in oil it dries very badly indeed. Although it has been recommended as a pigment, dragons' blood does not merit the attention of the artist.

Chapter Ten - Orange Pigments

The few orange pigments we possess are, on the whole satisfactory, both in respect of colour and permanence. These can be supplemented to any extent by mixtures of permanent red with permanent yellow.

Cadmium Orange

Was first introduced to the art world at the International Exhibition of 1862. It is an exceptionally brilliant and lustrous pigment, and is quite free from any rankness or harshness of colour. It is a simple original pigment, containing no base but cadmium; and is perfectly permanent, being quite unaffected by exposure to light, air, damp, or sulphuretted hydrogen; or by admixture with other pigments. In common with the cadmium yellows, it has a certain amount of transparency, and is invaluable for gorgeous sunsets. It is of great depth and power in its full touches, and the pale washes are marked by the clearness and delicacy which are so essential in painting skies. In illumination cadmium orange supplies a want which was formerly much felt.

Chrome Orange

Or *Orange Chrome* is, like chrome red, a basic chromate of lead. Like all the chromates of lead it is characterized by power and brilliancy; but also by rankness of colour, want of permanence, and a tendency to injure organic pigments. By reason of its lead base it is apt to be discoloured by sulphuretted hydrogen; but is on the whole preferable to the chrome yellows, being liable in a somewhat less degree to their changes.

Mars Orange

Is a subdued orange of the burnt sienna class; but without the brown tinge that distinguishes the latter. It possesses great clearness and purity; and considerable transparency. It affords bright sunny tints in its pale washes, and combines very effectively with white. Being, like Mars red, and Mars yellow, an artificial oxide of iron, it is more chemically active than the native ochres, and needs to be cautiously used with pigments affected by iron, such as the lakes of cochineal and intense blue. It is very permanent, and dries well.

Burnt Sienna

Is prepared by calcining raw sienna. It is a brown-orange, or orange-russet colour; and is richer, deeper, and more transparent than the raw earth. It also works and dries better. In all other respects it has the properties of raw sienna.

Burnt sienna is a very permanent, and generally serviceable pigment. It has, perhaps, a slight tendency to darken by time.

Burnt Roman Ochre

Is obtained by calcining a very bright Roman ochre. By this operation it acquires transparency and depth of colour.

It is moderately bright, forms good flesh tints with white, dries and works well both in water and oil, and is very permanent.

Burnt Roman Ochre is only used as an oil colour, and is nearly obsolete.

Neutral Orange

Or *Penley's Neutral Orange,* is a permanent compound pigment composed of cadmium yellow and Venetian red. It is chiefly valuable in watercolour, and is recommended as a first wash to break the extreme brilliancy of the paper, and to fix the pencil sketch.

Chapter Eleven - Yellow Pigments

The ancient painters seem to have been rather badly off for yellows, and in many old paintings and illuminations, glowing with vermilion and ultramarine, the place of yellow was supplied by gilding. Now, however, good yellow pigments are more numerous than those of any other colour.

Aureolin

Is also known as *Cobalt Yellow.* It is one of the most recent additions to the artist's palette and is a double nitrite of potassium and cobalt. It is permanent, transparent, possesses great richness of colour, and is the nearest approach to a perfect yellow in existence. In point of hue it more closely resembles the yellow of the spectrum than any other pigment. Aureolin is entirely unaffected by sulphuretted hydrogen, and, even in its faintest tints, is unaltered by exposure to the direct rays of the sun for a lengthened period. With all other colours it mixes safely and readily. In water colour it affords beautiful transparent tints, the paler washes being very clear and delicate. In oil, water, or fresco, it is equally eligible; but it cannot be used in enamel, as the colour is destroyed by great heat.

Cadmium Yellows

These are of comparatively recent introduction, the metal itself not having been discovered till 1818. They are sulphides of cadmium, and are consequently unaffected by sulphuretted hydrogen.

Deep Cadmium

Is a lustrous, glowing, orange-yellow. It is not very transparent; but is wonderfully clear and bright, and is the richest and most powerful yellow we possess. It works and washes well, and readily throws all other yellows into the shade when used alone.

Deep cadmium is permanent both with respect to sulphuretted hydrogen, and exposure to light and air. By admixture with white it gives a series of beautiful tints. It has been stated that the colour is destroyed by white lead. Theoretically this might very well happen; practically, if the cadmium be carefully prepared, and free from excess of sulphur, it does not. In fact, a good sample of cadmium yellow may rather advantageously than otherwise be compounded with white lead, for it is found that a mixture of equal weights of the two pigments will bear an atmosphere of sulphuretted hydrogen that completely blackens the white alone.

A steel palette knife should not be used with the cadmium yellows.

Pale Cadmium

Is not strictly pale; but pale only when compared with the preceding. It is, in fact, a full rich colour, brilliant and permanent; but without that tendency to orange which distinguishes the deep variety.

Chrome Yellows

These are chromates of lead, the hue depending on the proportion of chromic acid to. oxide of lead. They are of modern introduction; but from their want of permanence have been to some extent superseded by the cadmium yellows. They rival the cadmiums in brightness; but do not possess the mellow richness of those pigments.

Deep Chrome

Is a brilliant deep yellow with great opacity and body; but possesses a peculiar harshness and hardness of colour, which is apt to produce a coarse and disagreeable effect. Although it resists the sun's rays for a lengthened period, yet after some time it loses its original hue. In an atmosphere containing sulphuretted hydrogen it is changeable even to blackness. With many pigments it cannot be mixed without producing serious changes, particularly Prussian and Antwerp blues, which are ultimately destroyed.

Chrome Yellow

Is similar in all respects to the above; but is more lemon in hue.

Citron Yellow

Is chromate of zinc, and is a bright, pale, lemonlike yellow, slightly soluble in water. It is not affected by sulphuretted hydrogen; but does not preserve its colour on exposure to light and air, or even when kept in a book. In contact with organic substances it is liable to turn green. In this chromate as in many others, the affinity of the chromic acid for the base is small; and the former is liable to separate from the latter, and, by deoxidation, to become converted into green oxide of chromium.

Strontian Yellow

Was originally a chromate of strontium, a compound slightly soluble in water, and not more stable than chromate of zinc. The pigment, however, now sold as strontian yellow, is usually a mixture which resembles the original colour; but contains no strontium whatever. It is a light and delicate primrose colour, and possesses a durability to which the original could lay no claim.

Lemon Yellows

These consist essentially of chromate of barium. They are exceedingly difficult to make well, and upon the mode of manufacture depends not only the beauty of the colours, but also their stability. Properly and carefully prepared, chromate of barium is perfectly permanent; and is the only chromate which can be called so.

Lemon Yellow

Is of a vivid lemon hue, very pure and clear, and entirely free from the slightest tinge of orange. It has not much power, and is semi-opaque.

Lemon yellow works pleasantly both in oil and water, washes well, and is admirably adapted for glazing. It is not liable to change by the action of damp or foul air, by exposure to light, by contact with the steel palette-knife, or by mixture with white lead and other pigments. Being uninjured by lime it is eligible in fresco.

Pale Lemon Yellow

Is more of a primrose hue than the preceding, and precisely similar in its chemical and artistic properties.

Orient Yellow

Is one of the most recently introduced pigments. Though not so transparent as aureolin it is distinguished by greater richness and depth. It is of a soft golden hue, lustrous, and luminous, and resembles a brilliant and somewhat opaque Indian yellow. A gorgeous substitute for that fugitive pigment is produced by compounding orient yellow with aureolin.

Being more transparent than the cadmiums it is admirably adapted for sunset effects.

Orient yellow stands well in oil, and is quite unaffected by sulphuretted hydrogen. It cannot, however, be used as a water colour.

Kings' Yellow

Or *Orpiment,* is sesquisulphide of arsenic. It is found native in China and elsewhere, and was the *Auri-pigmentum* of the Romans, whence the present corrupt form.

It is a bright yellow pigment, and although not affected by sulphuretted hydrogen, is not durable either in water or oil. It is destroyed by being mixed with any of the lead colours; and, in fact, can only be safely used in an unmixed state.

Orpiment is not an eligible pigment, and is a very deadly poison.

Naples Yellow

Was formerly a compound of the oxides of lead and antimony, prepared at Naples. What is now sold as Naples yellow is a compound pigment, which in colour is an imitation of the original, and possesses the advantage of being perfectly durable and trustworthy. It is of a pleasing, light warm yellow hue; is opaque, and of good body.

Naples yellow may be readily and accurately imitated by mixing deep cadmium yellow with white.

Mars Yellow

Is an artificially prepared iron ochre, of the nature of raw sienna. In its general qualities it resembles the ochres; but is more transparent, as well as purer, richer, and brighter in colour. It is also more chemically active, and so should be used cautiously with pigments likely to be affected by iron. Like the ochres it is absolutely permanent, and is a good drier.

Raw Sienna

Is a ferruginous native pigment, of rather an impure yellow colour. It possesses more body and transparency than the ochres; but, unless skilfully prepared, has the objection of being somewhat pasty in working. It is not liable to change by the action of either light, time, or impure air; and may be safely employed in oil, water, or fresco.

The Ochres.

Those principally used by artists are known as *Yellow Ochre, Roman Ochre, Transparent Gold Ochre,* and *Brown Ochre.* They are native earths consisting chiefly of silica and alumina coloured by sesquioxide of iron. They are among the most ancient and permanent of pigments, and sometimes occur in the natural state, of so fine a quality that they require no preparation except washing.

In these pigments the sesquioxide of iron is in combination with silica and alumina, and so is less chemically active than in the artificial iron colours.

Yellow Ochre

Is a tolerably bright yellow of no great force. It is not affected by ordinary light, or by the action of sulphuretted hydrogen; but is somewhat darkened by time, and the direct rays of the sun.

It may be safely mixed with pigments which are themselves permanent; but with carmine and the cochineal lakes, or with intense blue, it should not be employed.

For fresco painting, yellow ochre is admirably adapted.

Roman Ochre

Is rather deeper and more powerful than the preceding, as well as more transparent and cooler in hue. In all other respects it is similar to yellow ochre.

Transparent Gold Ochre

Resembles Roman ochre; but is clearer in its tints and more transparent. It approaches the character of a clear, bright, raw sienna; but is purer and more brilliant.

Brown Ochre

Is a dense, deep-toned, brownish-yellow, which covers well without being too opaque. In its chemical characters it is similar to the rest of the ochres.

Quercitron Lakes.

Comprise *Yellow Carmine, Italian Pink,* and *Yellow Lake.* They are prepared by precipitating the colouring matter of quercitron bark with alumina. Quercitron bark is obtained from the *"Quercus tinctorial"* a kind of oak indigenous in North America. The colouring matter exists in the bark as a glucoside, i.e. in combination with glucose. This glucoside has been termed *Quercitrin.*

Yellow Carmine

Sometimes sold under the name of *Yellow Madder,* is the most concentrated lake prepared from Quercitron Bark. It is very rich, powerful, and transparent; but does not resist the action of light, and dries rather badly.

If it could only be depended on, yellow carmine would be of great value in glazing.

Italian Pink

Contains more alumina and less colouring matter than the preceding pigment, and is consequently not so rich and powerful, but is in other respects similar.

Yellow Lake

Is a still weaker preparation. It resembles Italian pink, but is more lemon in hue.

Gamboge

Is principally obtained from the *gokathu* tree in Ceylon and Siam. It is a gum-resin which exudes from the wounded leaves and young shoots.

Gamboge is a bright transparent yellow; but has no great depth. In its deepest touches it shines too much and verges on brown.

When properly used it is more durable than is generally reputed both in water and oil; and when mixed with other colours conduces to their stability, and helps them keep their place. It is deepened to some extent by impure air, and somewhat weakened by the action of light. In water it works remarkably well; but is with difficulty employed in oil in the dry condition.

Gamboge may be rendered diffusible as an oil colour by forming it into a paste with water, and mixing it with lemon yellow. The best method is, however, to combine it with alumina.

Extract of Gamboge

The pigment now known as 'Extract of Gamboge' is a compound of gamboge and alumina.

Indian Yellow

Is a pigment which has long been employed in India under the name *"Purree"* but has only in modern times been introduced into Europe. It consists of euxanthate of magnesia, and is obtained from the urine of the camel. It has a beautiful pure yellow colour, and light powdery texture; is of greater body and depth than gamboge, but is inferior in these respects to gallstone.

Indian yellow resists the sun's rays with singular power in water colour painting; yet, in ordinary light and air, or even in a book, the beauty of its colour is not lasting. In oil, both alone and in tint, it is decidedly fugitive. Owing, probably, to its alkaline nature, it has an injurious effect on carmine and cochineal lakes, when mixed with them.

Indian yellow works and washes admirably, and may be used in fresco.

Gallstone

Is a deep-toned, gorgeous yellow, affording richer tints than most other yellows; but it cannot be depended on for permanence, and therefore is seldom employed. Its colour is soon changed and destroyed by strong light, although not affected by impure air. In oil it is ineligible. True gallstone is an animal calculus formed in the gall-bladder of oxen; but the pigment sold under that name is often a substitute, resembling the original in colour, but of greater stability.

Chapter Twelve - Green Pigments

The green pigments in ordinary use are not very numerous; but when these are supplemented by mixtures of permanent blues with permanent yellows, we may regard our supply of greens as on the whole satisfactory.

Oxides of Chromium

The different varieties of sesquioxide of chromium are obtained by various methods, and both by wet and dry processes. They are either pale or deep, bright or subdued, opaque or transparent, according to the mode of production.

They are all strictly stable, being equally unaffected by exposure to light, air, or sulphuretted hydrogen. They can be mixed with other pigments without injury to themselves or to the pigments with which they are compounded. They are eligible both in water and oil, and dry well in the latter vehicle.

The varieties which are not hydrated can be used in enamel.

Oxide of Chromium

Or *Opaque Oxide of Chromium,* is found native in an impure state; but is always prepared artificially for the artist's use. It is obtained by dry processes, and consists of the anhydrous sesquioxide. It is a cold, sober sage green, deep-toned, opaque, and although dull, agreeable to the eye. Its tints with white are very delicate and pleasing.

Being very dense and powerful, it must be employed with care to avoid heaviness. In water colour it washes rather badly.

Transparent Oxide of Chromium

This pigment, being very deficient in body, is only eligible in oil. It is a very pale greyish green, in powder; but, ground in oil, it yields an agreeable yellowish-green of some depth, which is moderately bright, but not very pure or clear.

Viridian

Or *French Veronese Green,* is a very rich, deep, and transparent pigment. It is a hydrated sesquioxide of chromium containing two molecules of water. Its hue is of a bluish-green, its deepest shades verge on black, while its light tints are unsurpassed for clearness. No mixture of blue and yellow pigments will afford a green so beautiful and stable. Viridian is admissible in fresco; but cannot be employed in enamelling, for its colour depends on the water of hydration, which is expelled by strong heat.

Copper Greens

Comprise *Emerald Green, Malachite Green,* and *Verdigris.* They are characterized by brightness of colour, good body, and considerable permanence. When exposed to damp and impure air, they are ultimately blackened. They darken by time, dry well in oil, and are all more or less poisonous, even those not containing arsenic.

Emerald Green

Is an aceto-arsenite of copper. It reflects light very powerfully, and is the most durable pigment of its class, not being affected to an appreciable extent by damp, or by that amount of impure air to which pictures are usually subject. It works much better in water than in oil, and in the latter vehicle dries with difficulty. Bearing the same relation to greens that pure scarlet bears to reds, its vivid hue is almost beyond the scale of other bright pigments, and immediately attracts the eye to any part of a painting in which it may be employed. Where this colour is required, no mixture of blue and yellow will serve as a substitute.

Malachite Green

Or *Mountain Green,* occurs native in Cumberland, and consists of hydrated bicarbonate of copper, but malachite can be prepared artificially of a much finer colour than the natural variety. In both forms it withstands the action of light and air; but in common with the other non-arsenical copper colours, it is blackened by the combined action of damp and sulphuretted hydrogen. On the whole it cannot be recommended as a pigment.

Verdigris

Is a subacetate of copper, i.e. a compound of acetate of copper with oxide of copper. It is of a bright green colour inclining to blue.

Verdigris is the least durable of the copper greens. As a water-colour, it soon fades by the action of light and air, and is very susceptible to damp and sulphuretted hydrogen. In oil it is permanent with respect to light and air; but moisture and an impure atmosphere change its colour, and cause it to effloresce, or rise to the surface of the oil in spots. It dries rapidly, and is exceptionally useful with other greens or very dark colours. In varnish it stands better; but cannot be considered eligible either alone or compounded.

The Italian painters used this pigment, and the bright greens in many old pictures are produced by glazings of verdigris.

Chrome Green

The so-called c chrome greens; are compounds of chrome yellow with Prussian blue. They are often called *Brunswick Greens,* or *Cinnabar Greens,* and are fine bright colours, although quite unfit for the artist's craft. Chromate of lead has a chemical action on Prussian blue and ultimately destroys it.

Hooker's Green

Is a compound of Prussian blue and gamboge, these two pigments have about the same degree of stability, and are perfectly innocuous to each other. Hooker's green is more durable and transparent than the chrome greens which have just been described.

Prussian Green

Like the preceding is composed of Prussian blue and gamboge; but contains a very large excess of Prussian blue. It is consequently a bluish-green of the utmost depth and transparency, verging on black in its deep washes.

Sap Green

Is a pigment of vegetable origin, and is prepared from the juice of buckthorn berries, the green leaves of woad, etc. It is usually preserved in bladders, and is sometimes called *bladder green.* When good, it is of a dark colour and glossy fracture, extremely transparent, and is a fine natural yellowish-green. Sap green is sometimes employed in flower painting. It is, however, a very imperfect pigment, disposed to attract atmospheric moisture, and to get mildewed. Having little durability in water, and less in oil, it is not eligible in the one, and is totally useless in the other.

Terre Verte

Is a sober bluish-green with a gray cast. It is a species of ochre containing silica, protoxide of iron, magnesia, potash, and water. It is not bright or powerful; but is a very durable pigment, being unaffected by strong light or impure air, and combining safely with other colours. It has not much body, is semi-transparent, and dries well in oil. The different varieties of Terre Verte have been used as pigments from the earliest times. It is very useful in glazing, and Rubens availed himself of it largely for this purpose.

Terre Verte seems to get slightly darker in course of time, and should therefore be used rather cautiously.

Cobalt Green

Or *Rinman's Green* is a mixture of the oxides of zinc and cobalt, and is prepared by heating carbonate of zinc which has been precipitated with a small percentage of carbonate of cobalt. It is a moderately bright green, permanent both alone and compounded; but so sadly deficient in body and power as to have become almost obsolete. Rinman's green is an example of a pigment which is chemically good and artistically bad.

Chapter Thirteen - Blue Pigments

The painter will find that the number of good blues at his disposal is somewhat limited in comparison with the reds and yellows. A pigment which is permanent, but which otherwise has the attributes of Prussian Blue, is much to be desired.

Genuine Ultramarine

Also termed *Native Ultramarine,* and *Real Ultramarine,* is the most costly, most permanent, and most celebrated of all pigments.

It is obtained by isolating the blue colouring matter of the *Lapis-Lazuli,* a stone brought chiefly from China, Thibet, and the shores of Lake Baikal. There is little doubt that lapis-lazuli was the sapphire of the ancients.

Chemical analysis has shown that the colouring matter of lapis-lazuli consists essentially of silica, alumina, sulphur, and soda, and that the colour is probably due to sodium sulphide, and sodium thiosulphate.

Genuine ultramarine is prepared from the stone by a curious mechanical process, which, when well executed, separates the blue very perfectly from all extraneous matter, and yields first a deep and rich product, then a paler one, and lastly a bluish gray, which is known as *Ultramarine Ash.* The refuse, containing little or no blue, furnishes a useful pigment called *Mineral Gray.*

Genuine ultramarine, when of fine quality and skilfully prepared, is a most exquisitely beautiful blue, ranging from the utmost depth of shadow to the highest brilliancy of light and colour. It is transparent in all its shades, and leans neither to green on the one hand, nor to purple on the other. It is not injured by damp, by impure air, or by the intensest action of light; and is so eminently durable that it remains unchanged in the oldest paintings. It dries well, works well in oil and fresco, and may be safely compounded with all other pigments. In the representation of sky and atmosphere it is unapproached.

Though unexceptionable as an oil-colour, both in solid painting and glazing, it does not work so well as some other blues in water; and, unless carefully prepared, is not well adapted for mixed tints, on account of a gritty quality, of which no grinding will entirely divest it, which causes it to separate from other pigments.

Artificial Ultramarines

Comprise *Brilliant Ultramarine, French Ultramarine* or *French Blue, New Blue,* and *Permanent Blue.* The unrivalled qualities of native ultramarine prepared from the lapis-lazuli rendered it most desirable to obtain an artificial compound which, while possessing similar properties, could be produced in quantity, and at a less costly rate. The problem was first solved in 1828, by M. Guimet, who won the prize of £500 which had been offered in 1824 by the 'Sociéte d'Encouragement' of Paris.

The artificial ultramarines are darker and less azure than the natural varieties; but the superiority of the latter consists, not so much in their greater purity of colour, although this is considerable, as in their far greater transparency. The finest French ultramarine is brilliant, powerful, permanent, and nearly, but *only* nearly, transparent. Possessing in a subdued degree the characteristics and qualities of the genuine variety, it works, washes, and dries well; and, being unaffected by alkalies, is eligible in mural decoration.

Brilliant Ultramarine

Or *Factitious Ultramarine,* is a specially fine preparation of M. Guimet; and of all the artificial ultramarines, presents the nearest approach to the natural product in transparency, purity of colour, and chemical characteristics.

French Ultramarine

Or *French Blue,* is a rich deep colour; but less transparent and vivid than the preceding variety, which is preferable in unmixed tints. French blue is a generally useful colour.

New Blue

Is an artificial ultramarine, holding an intermediate position between French blue and permanent blue.

Permanent Blue

Is a pale ultramarine with a cobalt hue; and is probably, in spite of its name, less permanent than the deeper varieties. It stands in the same relation to French blue as Antwerp blue does to Prussian Blue.

Cobalt Blues

Comprise *Cobalt Blue, Cerulean Blue,* and *Smalt.* They are all obtained by the action of heat on mixtures of cobalt oxide with other metallic bases; and, with the exception of smalt, are very durable.

Cobalt Blue

Is obtained by calcining a mixture of alumina and basic phosphate of cobalt.

It was discovered in 1802 by M. Thenard. Though not possessing the body, transparency, and depth of ultramarine, it works better in water, and hence is a great acquisition. It resists the action of light; but its beauty declines by time, and it is greened and ultimately blackened by impure air. Cobalt blue dries well in oil, does not injure or suffer injury from other pigments, and may be used in enamel and fresco.

Cerulean Blue

Or *Coeruleum,* is a stannate of cobalt, i.e. a compound of the oxides of tin and cobalt.

This comparatively new pigment has the distinctive property of appearing a fairly pure blue by artificial light, tending neither to green on the one hand, nor to purple on the other.

This advantage, added to its permanence, has conferred upon it a popularity which its mere colour would scarcely have gained. It is a light and pleasing blue with a greenish-gray colour by day; but possesses little depth and richness, and is far excelled in beauty by a good cobalt blue. A certain chalkiness, moreover, detracts from its transparency, and militates against its use in water. Moreover it washes badly. It is in oil, and as a night colour, that cerulean blue becomes of service For scene-painting it is admirably adapted.

Smalt

Was discovered about 1540, in Saxony, and is a double silicate of cobalt and potassium. It is a vitreous compound, in fact a blue glass, and is a vivid and gorgeous violet blue. In consequence of its gritty texture it washes badly, and has little body. Both in water and oil its beauty soon decays. It is chiefly employed in illumination and flower-painting.

Prussian Blue

Was discovered accidentally in 1710, by Diesbach, a Berlin colour-maker.

It consists essentially of ferrocyanide of iron, and is a colour of vast body and wonderful transparency; it has a soft, velvety richness, and its deepest washes are so intense as to appear black.

Prussian blue borders slightly on green, a quality which militates against its use in skies and distances. It dries and glazes well in oil; but unfortunately cannot be called permanent, although it will last a long time under favourable circumstances. It fades under the action of a strong light; but regains its colour in the dark. Its colour, in fact, has the singular property of fluctuating under certain conditions, according to whether the surroundings are favourable for it to acquire or relinquish oxygen. It is darkened and discoloured by damp and impure air, and, as its colour is destroyed by high temperature and alkalies, it cannot be employed in enamel or fresco.

Antwerp Blue

Is similar in hue to Prussian blue, but is paler and less permanent. It is a compound of Prussian blue with alumina.

Cyanine Blue

Or *Leitch's Blue,* is a mixture of cobalt blue and Prussian blue. This pigment loses its colour by degrees when exposed to air and light, and gradually assumes the hue of the paler but more permanent cobalt.

Indigo

Or *Indian Blue,* was one of the pigments known to the ancients. It is chiefly derived from the leaves of various species of "Indigofera" which are found in India, Africa, and America.

Indigo, like the colouring principle of madder, does not exist as such in the living plant; but in the form of a glucoside called *Indican,* which is colourless. When, however, the leaves are plucked and macerated in water, a process of fermentation sets in, and the indican is decomposed, with the formation of indigo blue and glucose.

Indigo is not nearly so saturated in colour as Prussian blue; but is extremely powerful and transparent. It has great body, and works and glazes well both in water and oil. It is inferior in permanence to Prussian blue. Impure air has an injurious effect upon it, and in tint with white lead it is decidedly fugitive.

Intense Blue

Is indigo refined by solution and precipitation. By this process it becomes more durable, and is rendered much more powerful, transparent and deep. In other respects it possesses the properties of common indigo. It is, however, more apt to penetrate the paper on which it is employed.

Chapter Fourteen - Purple Pigments

We have, unfortunately, no purple pigment which is both permanent and saturated in colour. Tolerable purples may be obtained by mixing permanent reds with permanent blues.

Purple Madder

Is prepared from the madder plant, and is, like the rest of the madder colours, a lake formed by precipitating the colouring matter in combination with a metallic oxide. It is the most useful, and with the exception of Mars violet, the only permanent purple pigment. In colour it is a purple leaning to marrone; it is marked by soft subdued richness rather than by brilliancy, and affords the greatest depth of shadow without coldness of hue. It has great transparency and body, and neither gives nor sustains injury by admixture. It dries and glazes well in oil, works well, and is altogether a most eligible pigment.

Purple madder may be used in fresco, as it is quite uninjured by lime.

Purple Lake

This colour might almost be classed among the reds, as it is a species of crimson lake with a purple hue. It is transparent, deep-toned, and is useful in shadows. In its general properties it resembles crimson lake; but is on the whole more durable.

Burnt Carmine

Is obtained by partially charring carmine. It is a magnificent reddish-purple of extreme richness and depth. It is probably not more permanent than ordinary carmine.

Burnt Lake

Holds the same relation to crimson lake as burnt carmine to ordinary carmine. Hence it is a weaker variety of the preceding colour, with less richness and permanence.

Indian Purple

Is prepared by precipitating cochineal extract with sulphate of copper. It is a very deep-toned, but rather cold and subdued purple, which is apt to blacken on exposure to light and air.

Violet Carmine

Is obtained from the root of the *"Anchusa tinctoria"* and is a brilliant bluish-purple of much richness. On exposure to light and air it loses its colour and blackens.

Mars Violet

Like the rest of the Mars colours, is an oxide of iron. It resembles Indian red in body, opacity, and general properties, but is darker in colour. It is very permanent and dries well.

Chapter Fifteen - Brown Pigments

OUR list of brown pigments leaves nothing to be desired. They are very numerous, and are, almost without exception, characterised by great durability.

Brown Madder

Is a lake prepared from the madder root, and is an exceedingly rich marrone-brown of great depth and intensity. It affords the richest description of shadows, and in water-colour is especially indispensable. It is, like all the madder pigments, very permanent; it dries well, works very pleasantly, and altogether is a pigment which cannot be too strongly recommended to artists.

Rubens' Madder

Is also a preparation of the madder root. It is more russet in hue than the preceding, and is very pure, transparent, and permanent.

Although not employed so much as brown madder, it is an exceedingly serviceable pigment. It glazes admirably, but does not dry well in oil.

Bone Brown

Is obtained by partially charring ivory dust until it becomes of a brown colour. This pigment, although much esteemed by artists, is not very eligible. It is a bad drier, and will not withstand the action of strong light.

Bone brown is only used as an oil-colour.

Bistre

Is prepared from the soot of wood-fires, and is a very powerful citrine-brown, with a clearness about it suited to architectural subjects. It is only used as a water-colour, is perfectly durable, but has a tendency to condense the moisture of the atmosphere.

Prussian Brown

Is a compound of sesquioxide of iron and alumina, prepared by calcining an aluminous Prussian blue. It is an orange-brown, and resembles burnt sienna; but it is not so rich and powerful. It is transparent, permanent, and a good drier.

Burnt Umber

Is prepared by calcining raw umber. It is a quiet brown, with a deeper tone and more russet hue than raw umber. It works and washes well in water, dries rapidly in oil, and is perfectly stable in either vehicle. It is eligible in fresco.

Verona Brown

A pigment confined to oil-painting, is a calcined ferruginous earth. It is a very serviceable citrine brown.

Vandyke Brown

This pigment is a species of peat or bog-earth of a fine, deep, brown colour, and is semi-transparent. The original brown used by Vandyke was an earth brought from Cassel. The Vandyke brown of the present day is a bituminous ochre purified by washing and grinding. It is apt to vary in hue, is durable both in water and oil; but, like all bituminous earths, dries tardily in the latter vehicle.

Vandyke brown forms clear pale tints, and deep and glowing shadows. In water it sometimes has the bad property of working up, and when it is necessary to lay on a large body of colour the moist tube colour should be preferred to the cake.

Caledonian Brown

Is a permanent native pigment, which is only used in oil-painting. It is a magnificent orange-russet brown of considerable transparency, and is marked by great richness and depth.

Cappah Brown

Is likewise a pigment peculiar to oil-painting. It is a species of bog-earth containing peroxide of manganese, and is found at Cappah near Cork. It varies considerably in hue; but always possesses more or less richness and transparency.

Cappah brown works very well in oil and varnish, dries promptly, but does not keep its place.

Cologne Earth

Was originally a native bituminous earth; but the pigment now known under the name is prepared by calcining Vandyke brown, and is more permanent than the original variety. It is similar in general properties to Vandyke brown, but deeper in colour.

Asphaltum

Or *Bitumen,* is a variety of pitch which rises to the surface of the Dead Sea, concretes by the action of the sun and atmosphere, and, floating to the shore, is gathered by the Arabs.

The pigment now known as asphaltum is prepared artificially by distilling resinous and bituminous matter, and is obtained in great abundance as a bye-product in the manufacture of coal-gas. It is chiefly confined to oil-painting, and its fine brown colour and perfect transparency lure many artists to use it freely, notwithstanding the certain destruction that awaits the work in which it is much employed. Changes in temperature and atmospheric condition cause it to contract and crack, and it has a tendency to blacken. It is, in fact, to be regarded rather as a dark varnish than as a solid pigment.

It is common to call the solution in turpentine *Asphaltum,* and the mixture with drying oil *Bitumen.* A preparation for the use of watercolour artists is employed under the name of Liquid *Asphaltum.*

Mummy

Is a bituminous product mixed with animal remains, brought from the catacombs of Egypt, where, three thousand years ago, liquid bitumen was employed in embalming.

It resembles asphaltum in its general qualities, and is often substituted for it as being less liable to crack or move on the canvas.

Mummy varies exceedingly in its composition and properties, and but little reliance should be placed upon it. It is only used as an oil-colour.

Sepia

Is named after the cuttle-fish, *"Sepia officinalis"* from which it is obtained. All the species of cuttle-fish are provided with a dark-coloured fluid, which they emit to obscure the water when they wish to escape from danger, or to seize their prey. This liquid consists of a mass of extremely minute carbonaceous particles mixed with an animal gelatine, and is so concentrated that an ounce of it will darken many thousand ounces of water.

Sepia is a powerful dusky brown of fine texture; it is transparent, works admirably in water, combines well with other pigments, and is very permanent. It is extremely clear in its pale tints, and is perhaps the best washing pigment we possess.

Sepia cannot be used as an oil-colour, as it dries very reluctantly.

Warm Sepia

Is the natural sepia warmed by mixing it with browns of a red hue.

Roman Sepia

Is a similar preparation to the preceding, but with a yellow instead of a red tendency.

Chapter Sixteen - Citrine and Olive Pigments

CITRINE and olive are very poorly represented on the palette. Our best citrine is not permanent, and we have no stable olive pigment.

Fair citrine and olive colours may be produced in great variety by mixing permanent green and orange pigments, and permanent green and purple pigments, respectively.

Brown Pink

Or *Stil-de-Grain,* is generally prepared from Avignon berries (seeds of the *rhamnus infectorius*) or from Turkey and Persian berries; (*rhamnus amygdalinus*) but is sometimes made from quercitron bark. If produced from the berries it must be branded as fugitive; but if obtained from the bark it may be termed semi-stable. In either case it is a lake precipitated by alum from a decoction of the colouring matter containing a great excess of alkali.

The colouring principle of the berries has been called *Rhamnatin.* It exists, however, combined with glucose as the glucoside *Rhamnin,* but the decomposition is easily effected by chemical reagents.

Brown pink is a fine rich citrine colour with much richness and transparency. It works well in both water and oil. In thin glazing it will not stand, and the tints with white lead are very fugitive. The variety made from berries dries badly.

Raw Umber

Is a natural ochre, and is a hydrated silicate of iron, manganese, and alumina.

It was first brought from ancient Ombria (the modern Spoleto), in Italy, but the best now comes from Cyprus, and is called "Turkish" or "Levant umber."

Raw umber is of a fine brownish-citrine colour. It is semi-opaque, dries rapidly, and does not injure other pigments by admixture. By time it grows darker; but this disadvantage may to some extent be eliminated by mixing it with pigments of similar hue which pale on exposure.

Mars Brown

Is either a natural or artificial ochre containing iron, or iron and manganese.

It is a rich and strictly permanent pigment, which is similar to raw umber; but more orange in hue.

Olive Lake

Is exclusively an oil-colour. Originally it was a lake prepared from the green ebony. This variety, however, is now obsolete, and its place has been supplied by a mixture which is semi-stable, and liable to blacken.

Olive Green

Sometimes called *Dewint's Green,* is an arbitrary compound, or mixed green, of a fine deep olive colour, and sober richness. It is only used as a water-colour, olive lake supplying its place in oil. Like many other compound pigments, it is either permanent, semi-stable, or fugitive, according to the constituents of which it is composed. Generally speaking it is more beautiful than durable, and often is decidedly fugitive, fading on exposure to light and air.

Chapter Seventeen - Gray Pigments

There is hardly any necessity for gray pigments, so readily are they obtainable by admixture. The following, however, have found a place on the palette.

Ultramarine Ash

Is, as already stated, obtained from the *"lapis lazuli"* after the richer and more intense blue has been extracted. It is a valuable bye-product of a pale azure gray colour which varies considerably in tone.

As a water-colour it washes much better than genuine ultramarine, and affords very delicate tints.

Mineral Gray

Is obtained from the *"lapis lazuli"* after the blue and ash have been extracted. It is, in fact, an inferior kind of ultramarine ash, and is a pale blue-gray. It possesses the permanence of ultramarine, and is a pigment peculiar to oil painting. It is useful in the representation of misty effects.

Neutral Tint

Is a compound shadow colour of a cool character. It is permanent, except that on exposure the gray is apt to become grey, a change which may be prevented by a slight addition of ultramarine ash.

Payne's Gray

Resembles the preceding in being a compound colour, and liable to become grey in course of time; but differs from it in being more lilac in hue.

Chapter Eighteen - Black Pigments

We have but few black pigments; but they are all permanent, both in oil and water colour, and meet in every respect the requirements of the artist. Our black pigments, like those of the ancients, are all derived from carbonaceous substances.

Ivory Black

Is obtained by charring ivory in closed retorts. When well-made it is the richest and most transparent of all the blacks, and is perfectly durable and eligible both in water and oil. If, however, insufficiently burnt, it is brown, and dries badly, and if too much burnt, becomes opaque and loses intensity. Ivory black is a full, silky black, and is serviceable where the sooty density of lamp-black would be out of place. It has a tendency to brown in its pale washes.

As, chemically speaking, ivory black is nothing more or less than animal charcoal, it is better not to bring it in contact with organic pigments. The powerful decolourising action of animal charcoal is well known, although no doubt gums and oils would retard the action. In compounding colours therefore, blue-black, and lamp-black should be substituted for ivory black.

Lamp Black

Is a smoke black, being the soot obtained by burning resins or resinous woods. It is a pure vegetable charcoal of fine texture, not quite so intense and transparent as ivory black, but less brown in its pale washes. It has a very strong body that covers readily every underlay of colour, works well, but in oil dries badly. Being a dense solid pigment, it should be used sparingly to avoid heaviness.

Blue Black

Is a well burnt and levigated charcoal prepared from vine twigs. It is of weaker body than ivory black or lamp black, and consequently better suited for many purposes; especially in landscape, where a black and sooty effect is to be avoided. In common with all the carbonaceous blacks it has a preservative influence on white lead. If white lead be mixed with a small proportion of blue black, and washed over with zinc white, it may be exposed to any ordinary impure atmosphere with comparative impunity.

Cork Black

Is a soft black obtained by charring cork; it is a blue but not a velvety black, and should not be used when intensity is required. It is chiefly valuable for mixtures.

Indian Ink

Or *Chinese Ink,* is brought from China in oblong cakes of a musky scent, ready prepared for painting in water. It varies considerably in body and colour.

The principal constituent of Indian ink seems to be a smoke black similar to our lamp black; a small percentage of camphor is present, and it has been stated by some authorities that sepia enters into its composition.

Indian ink is made into a solution for artists, to avoid the tediousness of rubbing on the tile.

Black Lead

Plumbago, or *Graphite,* is a species of carbon, and contains traces of iron, silica and alumina. The best blacklead is obtained from the Borrowdale Mine in Cumberland. As a water colour, blacklead may be effectively used in shading and finishing pencil drawings. In oil it possesses a remarkable covering property, forms a very pure grey, dries quickly, has no action on any colour, and endures for ever.

Blacklead has long been used for pencils and crayons; but only in recent years has been employed as a pigment.

Appendices

Tables Relative to The Permanence of Pigments

Table One – Pigments Affected by Exposure to Light and the Normal Atmosphere

RED	Pure Scarlet. Carmine. Crimson Lake. Scarlet Lake. Indian Lake. Dragons' Blood.
YELLOW	Kings' Yellow. Citron Yellow. Strontian Yellow. Yellow Lake. Italian Pink. Gamboge. Extract of Gamboge. Gallstone. Indian Yellow.
GREEN	Chrome Green. Hooker's Green. Prussian Green. Sap Green.
BLUE	Prussian Blue. Antwerp Blue. Cyanine Blue. Indigo. Intense Blue.
PURPLE	Purple Lake. Burnt Carmine. Burnt Lake. Violet Carmine. Indian Purple.
BROWN	Bone Brown.
CITRINE	Brown Pink.
OLIVE	Olive Lake. Olive Green.
GRAY	Neutral Tint. Payne's Gray.

Table Two – Pigments Affected by an Atmosphere Containing Sulphuretted Hydrogen

WHITE	Flake White. Cremnitz White. Blanc d'Argent.
RED	Pure Scarlet. Red Chrome.
ORANGE	Orange Chrome.
YELLOW	Deep Chrome Yellow. Pale Chrome Yellow. Naples Yellow.
GREEN	Chrome Green. Emerald Green. Malachite Green. Verdigris.
BLUE	Cerulean Blue. Cobalt Blue. Smalt. Cyanine Blue.
PURPLE	Indian Purple.

Table Three – Pigments which Suffer Change by Admixture with White Lead and Other Lead Compounds

RED . . .	Pure Scarlet. Carmine. Crimson Lake. Scarlet Lake. Madder Carmine. Rose Madder. Pink Madder. Madder Lake. Indian Lake. Dragons' Blood.
YELLOW . .	Kings' Yellow. Yellow Lake. Italian Pink. Gamboge. Extract of Gamboge. Indian Yellow. Gallstone.
GREEN. . .	Sap Green.
BLUE . . .	Indigo. Intense Blue.
PURPLE . .	Purple Lake. Burnt Carmine. Burnt Lake. Indian Purple. Violet Carmine.
CITRINE . .	Brown Pink.
OLIVE . . .	Olive Lake. Olive Green.

Table Four – Pigments which are Decomposed by Admixture with Ochres, and other Ferruginous Substances

RED	Pure Scarlet. Carmine. Crimson Lake. Scarlet Lake. Madder Carmine. Rose Madder. Pink Madder. Madder Lake.
YELLOW	Kings' Yellow.
GREEN	Emerald Green. Malachite Green. Verdigris.
BLUE	Indigo. Intense Blue.
PURPLE	Purple Lake. Burnt Carmine. Burnt Lake. Indian Purple. Violet Carmine.
CITRINE	Brown Pink.
OLIVE	Olive Lake. Olive Green.

Table Five – Permanent Pigments

Pigments which withstand the action of Light, of Atmospheric Oxygen and Moisture, of Sulphuretted Hydrogen, and which may be safely mixed with Compounds of Iron and Lead.

Colour	Pigments
WHITE	Zinc White. Chinese White. Permanent White.
RED	The Vermilions. Mars Red. Light Red. Venetian Red. Indian Red. Red Ochre.
ORANGE	Cadmium Orange. Mars Orange. Burnt Sienna. Burnt Roman Ochre. Neutral Orange.
YELLOW	Aureolin. Cadmium Yellows. Lemon Yellows. Mars Yellow. Raw Sienna. Yellow Ochre. Roman Ochre. Transparent Gold Ochre. Brown Ochre.
GREEN	Oxide of Chromium. Transparent Oxide of Chromium. Viridian. Terre Verte. Cobalt Green.
BLUE	Genuine Ultramarine. Artificial Ultramarines. New Blue. Permanent Blue.
PURPLE	Purple Madder. Mars Violet.

BROWN . . .	Brown Madder. Rubens' Madder. Bistre. Prussian Brown. Burnt Umber. Verona Brown. Vandyke Brown. Caledonian Brown. Cappah Brown. Cologne Earth. Asphaltum. Mummy. Sepia. Warm Sepia. Roman Sepia.
CITRINE . . .	Raw Umber. Mars Brown.
GRAY . . .	Ultramarine Ash. Mineral Gray.
BLACK. . .	Ivory Black. Lamp Black. Blue Black. Cork Black. Indian Ink. Black Lead.

Table Six – Pigments which will Stand Intense Heat, and are Hence Suitable for Enamel Painting

WHITE . . .	Zinc White. Permanent White.
YELLOW . .	Naples Yellow.
RED . . .	Mars Red. Light Red. Venetian Red. Indian Red. Red Ochre.
BLUE . . .	Cobalt. Cerulean Blue. Smalt.
ORANGE . .	Mars Orange. Burnt Sienna. Burnt Roman Ochre.
GREEN . .	Oxide of Chromium. Cobalt Green.
PURPLE . .	Mars Violet.
BROWN . .	Burnt Umber. Cologne Earth. Prussian Brown. Verona Brown.
BLACK. . .	Black Lead.

Table Seven – Pigments which withstand the Action of Lime, and are Eligible for Fresco Painting

WHITE	Permanent White.
RED	The Vermilions. Light Red. Venetian Red. Indian Red. Madder Lakes.
ORANGE	Cadmium Orange. Chrome Orange. Mars Orange. Burnt Sienna. Burnt Roman Ochre.
YELLOW	Aureolin. Cadmium Yellows. Lemon Yellows. Naples Yellow. Mars Yellow. Raw Sienna. Yellow Ochre. Roman Ochre. Transparent Gold Ochre. Brown Ochre. Indian Yellow.
GREEN	Oxide of Chromium. Transparent Oxide of Chromium. Viridian. Emerald Green. Malachite Green. Verdigris. Terre Verte. Cobalt Green.
BLUE	Genuine Ultramarine. Artificial Ultramarines. New Blue. Permanent Blue. Cobalt Blue. Cerulean Blue. Smalt.
PURPLE	Purple Madder. Mars Violet.
BROWN	Bone Brown. Bistre. Prussian Brown. Burnt Umber. Verona Brown. Vandyke Brown. Cologne Earth. Asphaltum. Mummy.
CITRINE	Raw Umber. Mars Brown.
GRAY	Ultramarine Ash. Mineral Gray.
BLACK	Ivory Black. Lamp Black. Blue Black Cork Black. Indian Ink Black Lead.

A Dictionary of Pigments Not in Ordinary Use, and of Synonyms of Pigments Described in Part Three

African Green. — Syn. Emerald Green.

Almagra. — A deep variety of Red Ochre found in Andalusia.

Almond Black. — *See Peach Black.*

Anotta or Annatto. — A fugitive yellow pigment of vegetable origin. Also called "Rocou," and "Terra Orellana."

Antimony Orange. — Sulphide of Antimony. Also called Golden Yellow. Fades on exposure.

Antimony Red. — Also Sulphide of Antimony. It is sometimes known as "Mineral Kermes," and is not permanent.

Antimony White. — Oxide of Antimony. Has not the body of white lead, and is turned yellow by sulphuretted hydrogen.

Antimony Yellow. — An obsolete deep variety of Naples Yellow, which was principally used in Enamel Painting.

Antwerp Brown. — Syn. Asphaltum.

Antwerp Red. — A variety of Red Ochre.

Archil Purple. — Prepared from Litmus but is too fugitive for artistic purposes.

Armenian Bole. — Syn. Red Ochre.

Arsenic Yellow. — Arsenite of Lead. It resembles Orpiment in its. general properties, and is very poisonous. Also termed "Mineral Yellow."

Azure. — Syn. Genuine Ultramarine. Also for Cobalt Blue and Smalt.

Azure Blue. — An artificially prepared Carbonate of Copper. It is blackened by sulphuretted hydrogen.

Barytic White. — Syn. Permanent White.

Berlin Blue— Syn. Prussian Blue.

Bice. — A native Copper Blue, also called "Terre Bleu," and "Iris."

Bismuth Yellow. — Chromate of Bismuth. It is very fugitive.

Bismuth Purple. — Bismuthic Anhydride. Unstable.

Black Ochre. — A native earth which is permanent, but artistically inferior to the artificial blacks. It is also known as "Prussian Black," and "Earth Black."

Blanc Fixe. — Syn. Permanent White.

Bleu de Garance. — Syn. Artificial Ultramarine.

Blue Ashes. — A hydrated basic Carbonate of Copper, prepared artificially. Found native as "Mountain Blue" in Cumberland.

Blue Ochre. — Hydrated Phosphate of Iron. Found in Cornwall. It is a durable but rather dull blue, and is not easily procured.

Blue Verditer. — Hydrated Oxide of Copper. Not permanent. Also called "Bremen Blue."

Bole. — Syn. Red Ochre.

Bone Black. — Similar to Ivory Black, but warmer in colour. It dries very badly.

Bremen Blue. — See *Blue Verditer.*

Bremen Green. — See *Green Bice.*

Bronze. — A species of Prussian Green.

Brown-Red. — Syn. Red Ochre.

Brunswick Green. — Syn. Chrome Green, also for Emerald Green. The name is also applied to Oxychloride of Copper.

Burnt Madder. — Obtained by charring Madder Carmine. It is a permanent and unexceptionable pigment; but is rather expensive.

Burnt Verdigris. — An olive-coloured Oxide of Copper, which dries well, but is ineligible.

Cadmium White. — Hydrated Oxide or Carbonate of Cadmium. A very beautiful white, which is deficient in body, and turns yellow in the presence of sulphuretted hydrogen.

Cadmium Red. — Sulphide of Cadmium. It is permanent, but is not required.

Carnagione. — An Italian Light Red.

Cassel Earth. — Syn. Vandyke Brown.

Cassel Green. — See *Manganese Green.*

Cassel Yellow. — See *Patent Yellow.*

Cassia Fistula. — A Citrine pigment of vegetable origin. It is now obsolete.

Ceruse. — A French variety of White Lead. It is also called "French White."

Chestnut Brown. — A Lake prepared from the horse chestnut. Also known as "Hypocastanum." It is now obsolete.

Chica Red. — Extracted from the leaves of a tree which grows in Central America. It is not permanent.

China White. — An earthy white pigment.

Chinese Blue. — Syn. Prussian Blue.

Chinese Lake. — Syn. Scarlet Lake.

Chinese Orange. — An aniline colour. Very fugitive.

Chinese Yellow. — Syn. Kings' Yellow.

Chocolate Lead. — A compound of the oxides of lead and copper, prepared by a dry process. It dries well but is blackened by sulphuretted hydrogen. It is sometimes known as "Marrone Red."

Citrine Lake. — Syn. Brown Pink.

Cobalt Pink. — A Compound of the oxides of cobalt and Magnesium.

Cobalt Purple — Phosphate of Cobalt. Poor, chalky, but very durable colours.

Cobalt Red — Phosphate of Cobalt. Poor, chalky, but very durable colours.

Cobalt Ultramarine. — Syn. Cobalt Blue.

Coelin. — Syn. Cerulean Blue.

Copper Brown. — Ferrocyanide of Copper. Not permanent.

Copper Red. — Suboxide of Copper. It is not permanent.

Cologne Yellow. — Or Jaune de Cologne. A compound of Chromate of Lead, Sulphate of Lead, and Sulphate of Barium. It is quite unfit for artistic use.

Copper Yellow. — Chromate of Copper; a very ineligible pigment.

Cullen's Earth. — Syn. Cologne Earth.

Damonico. — An obsolete Ochre. It, may be imitated by mixing Burnt Sienna with Burnt Roman Ochre. Is also called "Monicon."

Di Palito. — A Light Yellow Ochre.

Drop Gum. — Syn. Gamboge.

Dtjmont's Blue. — Syn. Smalt.

Dutch Pink. — Syn. Italian Pink.

Dutch Ultramarine. — Syn. Cobalt Blue.

Dutch White. — A White Lead containing a large percentage of Barium Sulphate.

Earth Black. — See *Black Ochre.*

Egyptian Brown. — Syn. Mummy.,

Elsner Green. — Prepared by precipitating the colouring matter of yellow dye-wood with Hydrated Oxide of Copper.

Enamel Blue. — Syn. Cobalt Blue.

English Green. — Syn. Chrome Green.

English Pink. — Syn. Italian Pink.

English Red.— Syn. Venetian Red.

Erlaa Green. — *See Green Bice.*

Field's Carmine. — Syn. Madder Carmine.

Field's Lake. — Syn. Madder Lake.

Field's Purple — Syn. Purple Madder.

Field's; Russet — Syn. Purple Madder.

Flemish White. — Sulphate of Lead. It has not the body of Carbonate of Lead.

Florentine Lake. — A variety of Scarlet Lake.

Frankfort Black. — Said to be made by charring the lees of wine. It is principally used in copper plate printing.

French White. — See *Ceruse.*

French Green. — Syn. Emerald Green.

Gelbin's Yellow. — Chromate of Calcium. It is soluble in water, and very fugitive.

Giallolino. — Syn. Naples Yellow.

Green Bice. — Also called "Green Verditer," "Bremen Green," and "Erlaa Green." It is hydrated Oxide of Copper, and is one of the least eligible of the Copper Greens.

Green Earth —Syn. Terre Verte.

Green Lakes. — Compounds of Prussian Blue with various yellow pigments.

Green Smalt. — Syn. Cobalt Green.

Green Verditer. — See *Green Bice.*

Gold Blue. — A rather dull blue, similar in composition to Gold Purple.

Gold Purple. — Or Purple of Cassius, is a compound of the oxides of Gold and Tin. It is not brilliant, but is a rich, powerful, and permanent colour. Since the introduction of Purple Madder it has become obsolete, except in Enamel Painting.

Gold Reds. — Red Lakes formed by precipitating colouring matters on Oxide of Gold. Much too costly to be eligible pigments.

Golden Yellow. — Antimony Orange.

Guignet's Green. — Syn. Viridian.

Haerlem Blue. — Syn. Antwerp Blue.

Hamburgh Lake. — Syn. Crimson Lake.

Hamburgh White. — A White Lead containing a large percentage of Barium Sulphate.

Hungary Blue. — Syn. Cobalt Blue.

Hungary Green. — Syn. Malachite Green.

Hypocastanum. — See *Chestnut Brown.*

Imperial Green. — Syn. Emerald Green.

Indian Ochre. — Syn. Indian Red.

Indium Yellow. — Sulphide of the rare metal Indium. It resembles Cadmium Yellow; but is at present far too expensive to be employed.

Iodine Pink. — An iodide of Mercury. It is very fugitive.

Iodine Scarlet. — Syn. Pure Scarlet.

Iodine Yellow. — Iodide of Lead. A brilliant but extremely fugitive colour.

Iris. — See *Bice.*

Iris Green. — Syn. Sap Green.

Iron Yellow. — Ferrous Oxalate. It oxidizes and changes colour on exposure. Mars Yellow is sometimes termed Iron Yellow.

Jaune de Cologne. — See *Cologne Yellow.*

Jaune de Fer — Syn. Mars Yellow.

Jaune de Mars — Syn. Mars Yellow.

Jaune Minerale. — A pale variety of Chrome Yellow made in Paris.

Kermes Lake. — Prepared from the *coccus ilicis* of Southern Europe. It is not so brilliant, and probably not more durable than the Cochineal lakes.

Krems White — Syn. Cremnitz White.

Kremser White — Syn. Cremnitz White.

Laque Minerale. — A French variety of Orange Chrome. The name is likewise given to Mars Orange.

Lazulite — Syn. Genuine Ultramarine.

Lazurstein. — Syn. Genuine Ultramarine.

Leaf Green. — Syn. Chrome Green.

Leithner's Blue. — Syn. Cobalt Blue.

Lemon Cadmium. — Or Mutrie Yellow, is a preparation of Sulphide of Cadmium. It fades too quickly to be of artistic value.

Liege Black. — Syn. Blue Black.

London White. — Syn. Flake White.

Madder Marrone. — Or Marrone Lake. An obsolete preparation, made from the madder root. It maybe imitated by mixing Brown Madder with a little Rose Madder and Blue Black.

Madder Orange. — A dull and non-permanent colour made from Madder. Also termed "Orange Lake."

Madder Yellow. — Also a preparation of the madder root, is a dull and unstable yellow.

Magenta. — An aniline colour. Fades rapidly.

Majolica. — A variety of Red Ochre.

Manganese Black. — Black oxide of Manganese. It is permanent and dries very rapidly.

Manganese Green. — Manganate of Barium. It is very unstable, and is also known as "Cassel Green."

Manganese Brown. — Sesquioxide of Manganese. It is durable; and dries admirably; but is deficient in transparency.

Marrone Lake. — See *Madder Marrone.*

Marrgne Red. — See *Chocolate Lead.*

Massicot. — Protoxide of Lead. It is a pale yellow which is rapidly blackened by sulphuretted hydrogen. It is principally used as a dryer.

Mauve. — An aniline colour. Fades rapidly.

Milory Green. — Syn. Chrome Green.

Mineral Black. — An impure variety of carbon of soft texture and grey-black colour, found in Devonshire. Very durable and dries well.

Mineral Blue. — Syn. Antwerp Blue.

Mineral Green. — A hydrated basic Arsenite of Copper. It is also called "Neuwied Green."

Mineral Kermes. — See *Antimony Red.*

Mineral Purple. — Syn. Mars Violet.

Mineral Yellow. — Syn. Yellow Ochre. See also *Arsenic Yellow* and *Patent Yellow.*

Minium. — See *Red Lead.*

Mitis Green. — Syn. Emerald Green.

Montpellier Yellow. — See *Patent Yellow.*

Modan White — Earthy Whites, perfectly permanent but inferior in body.

Morat White — Earthy Whites, perfectly permanent but inferior in body.

Monicon. — See *Damonico.*

Mountain Blue. — See *Blue Ashes.*

Mutrie Yellow. — See *Lemon Cadmium.*

Native Prussian Blue. — See *Blue Ochre.*

Native Green. — An impure Sesquioxide of Chromium, found native.

Neuwied Green. — See Mineral Green.

Nottingham White. — Syn. Flake White.

Ocre de Ru. — Syn. Brown Ochre.

Olympian Green. — Syn. Emerald Green.

Orange Lake. — See *Madder Orange.*

Orange Lead. — Similar to Red Lead in its composition and properties.

Orange Ochre. — Syn. Burnt Roman Ochre.

Orange Orpiment. — Disulphide of Antimony. It resembles Kings' Yellow, and is very poisonous. Is also called "Realgar."

Orange Russet. — Syn. Rubens Madder.

Oxford Ochre. — A variety of Yellow Ochre, found near Oxford.

Outremer. —Syn. Genuine Ultramarine.

Paris Blue. — Syn. Prussian Blue. Also for Cobalt Blue.

Patent Yellow. — Oxychloride of Lead. This pigment is also known under the names of "Turner's Yellow," "Montpellier Yellow," "Mineral Yellow," and "Cassel Yellow."

Pattison's White. — Hydrated Oxychloride of Lead.

Paul Veronese Green. — Syn. Viridian.

Peach Black. — An obsolete violet black which was made by charring the stones of fruit. Also called "Almond Black."

Pearl White. — Is (1) a basic Nitrate of Bismuth, which is blackened by sulphuretted hydrogen, (2) a preparation of mother-of-pearl, which is eligible only as a water-colour.

Pelletier's Green. — Syn. Viridian.

Permanent Green. — Syn. Viridian.

Persian Green. — Syn. Emerald Green.

Platinum Yellow. — A compound of Platinic Chloride with the chloride of an alkali metal. A rich, deep, transparent yellow which blackens on exposure. It is too expensive to be available as a pigment.

Prussian Black. — See Black Ochre. A pigment also called by this name is made by heating Prussian Blue without access of air.

Prussian Red. — Syn. Venetian Red.

Purple Black. — A durable but obsolete pigment, prepared from the madder root.

Purple Ochre. — Syn. Mars Violet.

Purple of Cassius. — See *Gold Purple.*

Purple Rubiate. — Syn. Purple Madder.

Queens' Yellow. — Basic Sulphate of Mercury. A beautiful lemon colour, which is, however, too fugitive to deserve attention. It is also known as "Turbith Mineral."

Realgar. — See *Orange Orpiment*

Reboulleau's Blue. — See *Schweinfurt Blue.*

Red Lead. — A compound of the Oxides of Lead in varying proportions. It is blackened by sulphuretted hydrogen, and is only fit for industrial purposes. Red Lead is also called "Minium" and "Saturnine Red."

Red Precipitate. — Mercuric oxide. It blackens on exposure.

Rocou. — See *Anotta.*

Roman Green. — A mixture of Prussian Blue with Italian Pink.

Roman Lake. — Syn. Crimson Lake.

Roman White. — A variety of White Lead.

Rose Pink. — Prepared by dyeing whiting with decoction of Brazil Wood. It is much used in paper staining; but is too perishable for artistic use.

Rouen White. — An earthy White.

Rouge. — A species of Carmine prepared from Safflower. It is a beautiful, rich, transparent colour, but exceedingly fugitive.

Royal Blue. — Syn. Smalt.

Rubens Brown. — A light variety of Vandyke brown. A very beautiful and durable colour.

Rubric Lake. — Syn. Madder Lake.

Ruddle. — Syn. Red ochre.

Russet Rubiate. — Syn. Rubens Madder.

Sandal Wood Purple. — A fugitive lake with a tin base prepared from Sandal Wood.

Sandarac. — A native orange Sulphide of Antimony employed by the Ancients.

Satin White. — A compound of Sulphate of Calcium with Alumina.

Saturnine Red. — See *Red Lead.*

Saunder's Blue. — A copper blue.

Saxon Blue. — Syn. Smalt

Saxon Green. — Syn. Emerald Green.

Scarlet Ochre. — Syn. Venetian Red.

Scheele's Green. — An Arsenite of Copper prepared by precipitation. It is deeper than Emerald Green, but otherwise similar in properties; and is also known as "Swedish Green."

Schweinfurt Blue. — Also called "Reboulleau's Blue," is an Arseniate of Copper.

Schweinfurt Green. — Syn. Emerald Green.

Sil Atticum. — An ancient Red Ochre.

Silk Green. — Syn. Chrome Green.

Silver Red. — Chromate of Silver. It is. very fugitive.

Silver White. — Syn. Blanc d' Argent.

Sinoper. — The ancient name for Red Lead.

Spanish Brown. — A native Ochre.

Spanish Ochre, — Syn. Burnt Roman Ochre.

Spanish Red. — A variety of Venetian Red.

Spanish White. — An earthy White pigment.

Spruce Ochre. — Syn. Brown Ochre.

Stone Ochre. — Very similar to Oxford Ochre. It is found in Gloucestershire quarries.

Sulphate of Lead. — See *Flemish White.*

Swedish Green. — See *Scheele's Green.*

Terra di Sienna. — Syn. Raw Sienna.

Terra Orellana. — See *Anotta.*

Terra Puzzoli. — See *Terra Rosa.*

Terra Rosa. — A Red Ochre found in Italy. Also called Terra Puzzoli.

Terra Sinopica. — An ancient Red Ochre found in Cappadocia.

Terre Bleu. — See *Bice.*

Thallium Yellow. — Chromate of the rare metal

Thallium. It is browned by sulphuretted hydrogen.

Thénard's Blue. — Syn. Cobalt Blue.

Thwaite's' Yellow. — Chromate of Cadmium. A very beautiful yellow which is too unstable to be of any value.

Tin White. — Hydrated Stannous or Stannic Oxide. It is very similar to Zinc White; but is inferior in body and permanence.

Troy White. — An earthy White.

Tungsten White. — Tungstate of Barium. It is more opaque than Zinc White; but is very deficient in body.

Turbith Mineral —See *Queen's Yellow.*

Turnbull's Blue. — A variety of Prussian Blue.

Turner's Yellow. — See *Patent Yellow.*

Uranium Green. — An Oxide of Uranium. A durable but dull colour.

Uranium Yellow. — Uranate of Sodium. A fairly eligible; but rather expensive pigment.

Venetian Lake. — Syn. Crimson Lake.

Venetian White. — A White Lead containing a large percentage of Barium Sulphate.

Venice Red — An Italian Red Ochre.

Verde Vessie. — Syn. Sap Green.

Vert de Zinc. — See *Zinc Green.*

Vienna Blue. — Syn. Cobalt Blue.

Vienna Green. — Syn. Emerald Green.
Vine Black. — Syn. Blue Black.
Viride Aeris. — Syn. Verdigris.

Yellow Madder. — True Yellow Madder is a dull and fugitive preparation of the madder root. But so called "Yellow Madder" is often Yellow Carmine.

Yellow Ultramarine. — Syn. Citron Yellow, and sometimes also for Lemon Yellow.

Zaffre. — Syn. Cobalt Blue.

Zinc Green. — Is (1) synonymous with Cobalt Green. (2) Mixture of Citron Yellow with Prussian Blue.

Zinc Yellow. — Syn. Citron Yellow.

www.ingramcontent.com/pod-product-compliance
Lightning Source LLC
LaVergne TN
LVHW050938080826
845145LV00004B/1312

* 9 7 8 1 7 8 9 8 7 1 1 8 0 *